M000083550

GRACE

WAYNE A. BARBER

GRACE

[Letting Jesus Be Jesus *in* You]

BROADMAN
& HOLMAN
PUBLISHERS

NASHVILLE, TENNESSEE

10-digit ISBN: 0-8054-4029-1
13-digit ISBN: 978-0-8054-4029-4

Published by Broadman & Holman Publishers
Nashville, Tennessee

Dewey Decimal Classification: 248.84
Subject Heading: BIBLE-STUDY \ CHRISTIAN
LIFE \ SELF-IMPROVEMENT—
RELIGIOUS ASPECTS

Unless otherwise noted, Scripture quotations are taken
from the Holman Christian Standard Bible®, Copyright
© 1999, 2000, 2002, 2003 by Holman Bible Publishers.
Used by permission. Other versions include: NASB, New
American Standard Bible, © the Lockman Foundation,
1960, 1962, 1963, 1968, 1971, 1972, 1973, 1975, 1977;
used by permission; and KJV, King James Version.

1 2 3 4 5 6 7 8 9 10   10 09 08 07 06 05

This book is dedicated to my precious family.

Diana, my wife, who has put up with me for thirty-six years and whom I love very much!

Steven, my son, as well as his wife, Ann, and their little daughter, Ellie.

Stephanie, my daughter, as well as her husband, Erik, and their two precious children, Hollen and Jonathan.

Acknowledgments

I would just like to thank Lawrence Kimbrough for the marvelous assistance in writing this book. Without him it would not have happened! I would also like to thank Dr. Spiros Zodhiates, who was a mentor to me for eighteen years when I was a pastor in Chattanooga, Tennessee. He will never know the love and respect I have for him. I would like to thank Dr. Stephen Olford, who is now with the Lord Jesus, for the inspiration and the marvelous insights I gained from his friendship, his preaching, and his books over the years. I would like to thank Roy Hession, the author of *The Calvary Road*, who is also with the Lord Jesus, for his mentorship in my life. I would like to thank Jack and Kay Arthur for their kind and gracious gift of allowing me to teach with Precept Ministries for many years. I would like to thank Major Ian Thomas for his faithfulness and inspiration in teaching the message of the "Saving Life of Christ" and how that impacted my life. I would like to thank my precious children, Stephanie and Steven, for their love and encouragement, and their time and effort in seeing this book become a reality. I would like to thank my precious wife who has loved me for thirty-six years unconditionally and has been my very best friend. Finally, I would like to thank my Lord Jesus for loving me in spite of myself and for sending His Spirit to live in me to do through me what I could never do!

Table of Contents

Preface   ix

1 Out of the Coat Closet   1
   Are You Putting On Christ or Just Putting On?

2 Biscuits for Jesus   23
   All the Goodness, Baked Right In

3 Legally Dead   45
   The Frustration of Living under Law

4 Picture Yourself Here   67
   Having a Blast Enjoying God's Blessings

5 Down Home with Jesus   91
   Appropriating What You Already Have in Christ

6 Matching Outfits   115
   Looking Good in the Garment of Christ

7 It's the Only Way to Fly   139
   Still Surrendering after All These Years

8 The Ultimate Open-Book Test   161
   Can a Person Ever Look Forward to Finals?

Afterthoughts: Grace at Work   181
A Special Word to Pastors and Church Leaders

Preface

Growing up in the Bible Belt in Roanoke, Virginia, I grew up understanding Christianity from a works perspective. It was all up to me!

"We'll Work Till Jesus Comes" was sung over and over in my boyhood church. I felt like I had to measure up to a standard that hung over my head every day—a standard that continued to frustrate me because I could never seem to reach it, even with all my most sincere efforts. It was like trying to climb a ladder but never being able to reach the top rung. It was like running up a wet, slippery hillside with no traction on my shoes.

This performance mentality carried into my life as a pastor. I was trying to please everybody, to be the best me that I could be, but to no avail. I was miserable! To say I was frustrated would be an understatement. There was just *no joy* to my life, only a cloud that hung over my head, the depressing conclusion that I was a failure and would never be anything else.

But God is so good! He didn't let me stay there forever.

My dear, departed brother, Roy Hession, author of nine Christian classics, came to speak in the church where I served as pastor in Mississippi. I sat and listened as he spoke, but it wasn't really him speaking; it was Christ speaking through him to me.

For the first time in my life, I was hearing that it was OK for me to admit I was a failure, that God had never said I could please Him in the first place. I began to realize why the Holy Spirit, the Spirit of Christ, had come to live in me: to do through me what I had already learned I could not do in my own strength.

I cried for three days until I thought I was going to dehydrate. Yet it was in those few days that my life was transformed. I began the journey of learning to rest in Christ, allowing him to live his life in and through me. I began to learn the joy of just being a conduit through which his life and power could flow.

Not long after this I heard Major Ian Thomas, and more of the picture became clear to me. That was over twenty-five years ago. And now the message of living grace, of Christ living His life in and through me, continues to heal and overwhelm me to this good day.

This is not a message that can simply be explained and rationalized, as though understanding it in our heads is enough to make it a reality in our lives. It is not something that can be *taught*; it must be *caught*! If it is not lived, it is not learned. You learn this message as you live it, circumstance by circumstance until it becomes the reflex of your life.

My purpose in writing this book to you is so that you might come to understand the joy of the Christian life . . .

• The joy of allowing Christ to do through you what you know you can't do.

• The joy of joining Him in what He is up to in this world.

• The joy of learning to rest from the weariness of trying to do things for Him in your own strength.

This book can go where I could never go, speaking to people whom I may never meet face-to-face. I assure you, these words are already bathed in prayer that they might accomplish what God wants them to accomplish in your life!

May you come to know both His *saving* grace and His *living* grace, and discover that they are one and the same thing . . . the only thing.

Wayne Barber
Albuquerque, New Mexico
2005

CHAPTER 1

Out of the Coat Closet

[Are You Putting On Christ or Just Putting On?]

———————

I'd be willing to bet that somewhere along the line (if not within the past twenty-four hours), you've looked around at your Christian life and thought: "There's no way I can do this! I'm not good enough. I'm not strong enough. I'm not *anything* enough! This is too hard. It's too impossible. I'm just not able to do it!"

If you haven't ever said that, I hope you will soon . . . because this is the cry of a person who's on the brink of a great discovery. Not until you reach this point can you fully listen to what God has been saying to you all along. As Ian Thomas put it:

I can't—God never said I could.

He can—and He always said He would.

———————

Or to put it another way:

The Christian life is not what we can do for Him.
It's what He can do in and through us.

Now I have no doubt that most Christians agree
with this statement in theory. But I don't think many of
them really believe that the Christian life can actually be
lived out this way. Whether from fear, past failure, over-
confidence, or whatever, life has proved to them that the
Christian pattern is one of trying and failing, starting and
stopping—just grinning and bearing it.

And for many of us, this is far too true. Because
when we work under the assumption that living for God
is totally up to us, being a Christian can be downright
depressing. I've been there. I know.

But I'm here to tell you, it doesn't have to be that
way.

Paul said we can have "confidence" as believers—
that we can live consistent, vibrant, day-after-day lives of
faithfulness and joy—as long as we understand where
our confidence lies. "Not that we are competent in ourselves to consider anything as coming from ourselves,
but our competence is from God. He has made us competent to be ministers of a new covenant, not of the
letter, but of the Spirit; for the letter kills, but the Spirit
produces life" (2 Cor. 3:5–6).

Oh, there's a lot going on in these verses. You might
want to read back over them, just to try to capture the
depth of meaning and truth inside. But of all the things
Paul bundled together in this short passage, one main
thing comes out. It's that last word—the one that's hard
to say without putting an exclamation point after it.

Life!

"Life" is a word that's sort of like a warm shirt coming right out of the dryer. It's like a big, deep whiff of sunshine on a crisp autumn morning in the woods. Everybody wants to be a person full of "life"—invigorated, refreshed, a bounce in their step, an easy smile, the ability to take things in stride without spinning out of control.

And this is what Christ has come to offer us: "life . . . in abundance" (John 10:10).

If that's true, then, the thing that steals life from us can never be our relationship with Christ. No, no. What "kills" us, what defeats us, what makes us unable to experience victory and peace in our Christian experience (according to 2 Cor. 3) is the "letter" of the law.

Please don't read over this too quickly because it is so key: *the Spirit gives life, but the law brings death.*

Death by Checklist

Now, we may not think we're under the law, not the way people in Bible times were. When we read the Scriptures, when we study passages that talk about all the trouble Jesus had with those sticks-in-the-mud who had rules for this and rules for that, we don't consider ourselves to be part of that bunch.

I mean, we're not living in a day and age when being hard and intolerant is as tempting as it once was. As a rule, our society is more sensitive than ever before about judging and criticizing and picking out the faults in other people. Oh, sure, we may think bad things about them in our heads! We may whisper it around the lunch table

behind their backs! But most of us don't want the reputa-
tion of the Pharisees and other do-gooders of the Bible.

Furthermore, we're not nearly as disciplined and
regimented as the religious zealots of the first century
were. We may be habitual about our workout routines or
our TV watching, but we're not likely to think it's a huge
deal if we miss Sunday school one week or get behind on
our tithing.

So are we really at risk of coming up under the law's
control anymore?

You'd better believe it.

• Whenever we think God owes us something
because we're such good people, we're appealing to Him
on the basis of the law.

• Whenever we fast and pray with the main purpose
of hoping God notices our fervor and sacrifice, we're
wanting Him to reward us by our keeping of the law.

• Whenever we brag about what the Lord showed
us in the Book of Nahum during our quiet time this
morning, we're calculating our importance by the standards of the law.

• Whenever we assume that our ministry of choice
is more important than anything else that's going on at
church, we're basing our assessment on the law.

• Whenever we cross another congregation off our
approved list simply because of their worship style, their
service times, or their pastor's haircut, we're judging by
the law.

• Whenever we conclude that God has turned His
back on us and can never forgive us for the sins we've
committed, we're forgetting that we've been freed from
the law.

So, yes, our rules and regulations look much different than the cleaning and cooking variety that was instituted in the Old Testament. We set benchmarks and minimum requirements that would have been totally foreign to the ancient Israelites.

But I don't care what kind of horse it rides in on: the law is the law is the law.

And it never gives life. All it can ever do is kill.

For many people today, to live the Christian life means to jump higher, to go faster, to strangle the devil, to win new converts, to give more money, to knock off sugar, to catch all the hot conferences, and a hundred other things.

That's funny, because for the apostle Paul—who was arguably the most powerful, effective Christian example and evangelist in human history—to live was Christ.

Period.

Now come on, doesn't that sound a lot simpler?

It's true: you cannot live the Christian life. But that's OK. Your life is Christ.

Life Inside the Coat

If you were to take a coat or a jacket out of your closet, place it on a hanger over the doorknob, and tell it to raise up its sleeve to shake your hand, what would it do?

It would do everything it's capable of doing, which is nothing.

But the moment you slip that coat on, the moment your arms and your body give it form and purpose, you can command that same sleeve to raise up, point forward, wave hello to a friend, or hand your wife a vase full of flowers. That once-lifeless coat is now full of life!

This simple illustration is the easiest way I know to describe what normal Christianity is supposed to be about. Certainly, no analogy is perfect. We're not *exactly* like the coat, since we do have a choice about whether to respond to God's nudges, tugs, and movement. Yet the principle comes through nonetheless. Christ has come to live in us. He has not only saved us from the power of sin in our past; He has also delivered us from the power of sin in our future. He has not only given us His *saving* grace but also His *living* grace. The life is not the coat; the life is *in* the coat.

Perhaps no one other than Jesus Himself defined and experienced this biblical truth more successfully through His life than the apostle Paul. That's not because he was somebody special. He was no superhero. He didn't have a lock on Christian living that's not available to ordinary folks like you and me.

So whenever people ask me what it means to live the Christian life, to personally apply God's living grace, I always take them to Paul . . . and to the Book of Philippians. Because in this short, little four-chapter letter, we find the answer to the question: Can a person actually live the Christian life?

Yes, he can. Yes, she can. I've seen it happen in the life of Paul.

Christ Is My Life: Philippians 1

Before we can even begin to understand the message of Philippians—before we can grasp this foundational truth that "to live is Christ"—we first need to see where Paul was located when he wrote this letter.

He was in prison. In Rome.

That's interesting to me because he *thought* he was going to Rome to preach. Back in Romans 1, he had said, *I can't wait to get to you so I can preach the gospel to you.* "I want very much to see you, that I may impart to you some spiritual gift to strengthen you" (Rom. 1:11).

Little did he know he would be coming to Rome in bonds, in shackles, in chains. He would be brought there because of a false accusation that would cost him five years of his life in prison.

So this is the context of Paul's letter to the Philippians—not a self-inflicted prison of sin and selfishness but a prison imposed upon him as a result of his love and surrender to the Lord Jesus Christ.

You've been in one of those prisons before, haven't you? Maybe you're there right now, in a prison of circumstances you cannot change.

You need to make a living, for example, and yet God has placed you in a work environment that's hostile to your Christian faith, where people make fun of you and ridicule you all the time.

You're married to an unbeliever, perhaps, or to someone who doesn't share your devotion to Christ, who doesn't support your desire to serve Him. Not every day feels like prison, of course, but things come up from time to time when the tension is almost more than you can bear.

Maybe you're being forced to endure a serious health crisis, or a financial pinch, or a specific set of problems that seem overwhelming to you and impossible to deal with. A lot of prisons don't come with walls and doors and bars. Yet in the midst of this, Paul says, *You are partakers of grace with me.* We are fellow prisoners with him. So we desperately need to hear what he has to say.

And what he says in verse 21 is the key—not only to this first chapter, not only to the Book of Philippians, but to this whole idea of "living grace."

"For to me . . ." I love that. He didn't say, *For to you* or *to somebody else.* He said, "For me, living is Christ."

Progressive Prisons

Your whole perspective changes when Christ is your life. You don't look at your circumstances the way you used to look at them. You don't look at your prison cell the way other people look at theirs. When Christ is your life, you're living totally under grace. It's not up to you anymore; it's Christ in you.

That's why Paul could say, "I want you to know, brothers, that what has happened to me has actually resulted in the advancement of the gospel" (Phil. 1:12). What an incredible statement!

The word *know* in this verse means "to know experientially" or "to be taught." I mean, back in Philippi, the believers didn't know what Paul knew. That's why he had to write and tell them what Christ was teaching him in his trials. They were probably having prayer meetings, begging God to get him out of jail. *How in the world,* they thought, *can Paul be a missionary for you, Lord, if he's off stuck in a prison somewhere?*

They didn't know.

But who says you can't be a missionary while you're in prison? Who says Christ can't be your life when your circumstances seem to be working against you? Paul wrote to tell them what he "knew"—what Christ had been showing him during his long period of confinement. Yes, Paul was stuck in prison, but through Christ he knew progress was being made because, as he said,

"My imprisonment in the cause of Christ has become well known throughout the whole praetorian guard and to everyone else" (v. 13 NASB).

How could Paul have ever hoped to make personal contact with this elite unit of Roman influence—as well as with many other men and women at the heart of "Caesar's household" (4:22)—if God hadn't sent him to Rome in chains, if he hadn't been considered dangerous, if he hadn't been a man who wasn't allowed out of their sight for one second?

Actually, we don't know exactly what kind of imprisonment Paul was enduring at this moment. This was most likely not the same kind of dungeon imprisonment he talked about while writing his two letters to Timothy. Perhaps it was some sort of house arrest or another kind of confinement. But since the word *imprisonment* in verse 13 can be translated as "chains," I personally believe he was chained to somebody at all times.

So get this mental picture of what was possibly happening to him every day.

Here comes this big, burly guard who works the seven-to-three shift, fresh from a good night's sleep. All of a sudden, the guy who's just worked the graveyard shift—the man he's coming to replace—runs up to him, his eyes bloodshot, his hands trembling. Sputtering, he says, "You're not assigned to that Paul fellow, are you?"

"Yeah, so what? I hear he's just some little wimpy guy."

"Man, don't believe it! I've just been chained to him for eight hours! And I'm telling you, you don't know what you're in for!"

The new daytime guard flexes himself a little bit, pats his fist against the open palm of his other hand, and says, "I'm not worried about him. He'd better worry about *me!*"

So he goes into the room where Paul is, chains his ankle to Paul's ankle, his wrist to Paul's wrist. And as soon as Paul hears that last little click . . .

"Well, glory, praise God! We've got a big day in front of us, so let's get started with a word of prayer." And for eight solid hours, Paul has got one of the biggest, toughest, meanest brutes in all of the Roman Empire on a string, like putty in his hands, stuck to him where he can't get loose. It's gospel time in the old town tonight! And this captive of the state has snagged another captive audience!

That's what living grace can do to your perspective.

Do you feel totally helpless under your current circumstances? Have you given up trying to live for Christ with all this trouble and turmoil swirling around you? Are you just conceding the next few weeks and months, looking forward to a day when things will finally settle down and you can start living for God again?

No, Christ is alive in you right now, right here, right where you are. When Christ is your life, everything is about Him, everywhere you are, every day you live.

Christ Is My Attitude: Philippians 2

There was a time in my life when I not only had a prayer list; I also had a prayer *hit list*. I'd say, "God, if you could take out these ten people, I believe we could have real revival in our church."

I'm serious. Sometimes we'd have a dear member of our congregation to die, and I'd look up to God and say, "Lord, you missed! You got the wrong one!"

I remember one woman in particular who was a leader in our women's ministry. She was always coming up to me, fussing at me for not talking up her missionary offering enough from the pulpit.

She'd say, "Preacher, we're never going to raise the money unless you get up in that pulpit and start pumping it!" And I'd kind of motion to God and say, "Lord, this one, You can take her anytime."

Well, one night I was preaching on the second chapter of Philippians—that great passage of Scripture about having "this attitude in yourselves which was also in Christ Jesus" (v. 5 NASB). And no sooner had we said the closing prayer, then here she came, hustling up to me from across the sanctuary. "Preacher, you didn't say anything about the offering!"

So I said, "All right. What was your offering goal last year?"

"Thirteen hundred dollars."

"What is it this year?" I asked.

"Thirteen hundred and *fifty* dollars."

And I said, "Well, do you think God might could afford an extra fifty dollars this year?"

I didn't really mean it exactly the way it came out. The Bible teacher in me would have liked to believe I was giving her a holy exhortation, reminding her about God's limitless ability to provide "above and beyond all that we ask or think" (Eph. 3:20). But the truth is, I was mad at her. And she was mad at me. We were both just digging our heels in, determined to make the other one bend to our will.

But driving home that night, fresh from my Philippians 2 message on Christ's humble, submissive attitude—(I hate it when God does this)—the words of my sermon kept coming back to me.

He reminded me about Jesus, who "emptied Himself" of His rights as God's Son and took "the form of a slave" (v. 7).

He reminded me what I'd said about Timothy, one of those rare, "like-minded" souls who could "genuinely care" for other people's welfare, the kind of person who didn't seek after His "own interests" but only "those of Jesus Christ" (vv. 20–21).

He reminded me of Epaphroditus, a nobody with a name like few other people in the Bible but a man who never stopped "longing" to serve Christ and minister to others, even when he was "sick" and "distressed" (vv. 25–26).

Wayne, the Lord seemed to be asking, *do you love this woman?*

"No. I don't even *like* her."

And it was almost like God said to me, *Well, thanks for being honest, but . . . I want you to choose to love her. Let me love her through you.*

That moment was the beginning of a radical change in my life. The differences between this woman and me didn't disappear overnight, but I can tell you that she became one of my best, most cherished friends. As time went on, whenever anyone had a critical word to say about me, she was among the first to come to my defense.

And when she died, I didn't wink toward heaven and thank God for taking better aim this time. Instead, I deemed it an honor to preach her funeral and experienced the tender joy of knowing that she had gone to glory as my dearly loved sister.

God had transformed our attitudes . . . hers and mine. He had loved on both of us through each other.

You're Impossible!

When you let Christ live "inside the coat" rather than trying to do His work without Him, you're going to see people differently. You'll start looking at them through *His* eyes, not yours.

When Christ is your "life," He can also become your "attitude."

I mean, there's no way in the world you can obey a verse like this by yourself: "Do nothing out of rivalry or conceit, but in humility consider others as more important than yourselves" (Phil. 2:3). Do nothing? Not one selfish thing? Not one "desire for personal praise" (which is what the word translated "conceit" means)? Human beings are just not capable of that.

Here's another one: "Everyone should look out not only for his own interests, but also for the interests of others" (v. 4). Your flesh does not wake up in the morning wanting to do this.

And then there's the attitude of Christ "who, existing in the form of God, did not consider equality with God as something to be used for His own advantage. Instead He emptied Himself by assuming the form of a slave, taking on the likeness of men. And when He had come as a man in His external form, He humbled Himself by becoming obedient to the point of death—even to death on a cross" (vv. 6–8).

This is so critical. The attitude Christ had wasn't a one-time thing. It wasn't an every-now-and-then thing. It was a steady, consistent, present-tense, day-in and day-out experience.

And the Bible says we're to have this same kind of attitude ourselves. But we can forget about ever having it . . . unless Christ has become our attitude.

Now you won't submit to Him perfectly every time. You'll get angry with other people. You'll feel betrayed and put upon. The perfect comeback to someone else's remark will make a mad dash from the top of your brain to the tip of your tongue, and you'll choose to take charge of your attitude again.

But when you fail—when your old, selfish, want reflex kicks and screams and demands satisfaction—come running right back to the place where you can say, "Oh, God, you're exactly right. I trusted myself instead of you. I blew it big time! But Lord, I'm surrendering myself to You afresh, to let You be in me what only You can be."

You have to want *His* life, not yours. You have to be able to say to Him, "I want *Your* attitude, not mine."

That's what God wants to do in all of our relationships: to transform that attitude of ours that can never, ever, put others first or operate from genuine love. He wants to build in us a concern and compassion for others that begins inside with Him and animates His actions through us.

Sound impossible? It is.

But nothing is impossible with God.

Christ Is My Goal: Philippians 3

The Philippians had a problem. And nobody knew it more intimately or with more personal experience than Paul himself.

Paul, you remember, had once been part of an ultra-religious sect in Jewish life known as the *Pharisees*—a name that came from a Hebrew word meaning "to separate." Their role as experts and enforcers of the tiniest details of Jewish law was an intentional attempt to "separate" themselves from others, to show themselves superior to those who couldn't keep up with the code the way they could.

That was their goal: to set themselves apart, to outdo and outperform, to catch those who weren't toeing the line, and to wield control by setting them straight.

So like an ex-member of the mafia, who's able to tip off his innocent friends to the tactics of the enemy, Paul warned the Philippians to watch out for those who were Pharisees in tone, even if not in name.

Not that Paul minded tagging them with some names of his own, like:

• *"Dogs"*

Dogs in Paul's day often traveled in packs, preying on young, tender flesh. And just like the wolves who circled the towns of the first century, these crafty scavengers had crept out of the bushes and into the Philippian church, eager to pick off the young believers who were embracing Paul's "lawless" message.

• *"Evil workers"*

They may not have *looked* evil. They may not have seemed sinister on the surface. But "evil" was the blunt, accurate description for the raw-boned motivation of their hearts. And it still is today. The list of add-ons people try to place on top of authentic Christianity can sometimes appear to be good and constructive, but it's more evil than we realize. Paul had seen it up close, and he knew evil when he saw it.

• *"False circumcision"*

Most of these people Paul was talking about were proselytes who had converted to Judaism later in life. To do so, a person needed to be circumcised as an adult, in order to conform to the standards of the law. But no external act or ritual—either of the *physical* flesh or the *sinful* flesh of man—is able to purify the heart. Religion can dress up the outside, but only Christ can cleanse the inside.

Religion is built on the concept of accomplishment. "We can do it! We can do it! We can get a committee together, come up with a plan, and figure everything out. If people don't come along with us, we'll kick in the guilt. We'll make them feel so bad about themselves, it'll force them to get with it and help us get this done."

Have you ever seen that happen in the church? That's religion at work. That's a group of individuals placing themselves above others and loving every minute of it.

These people who had infiltrated Philippi smelled blood in the water. They fed off the power of control, the rush of religious authority.

But Paul knew their goal too well. It had once been his.

It's Who You Know

There was a time in Paul's life—long before he was able to say, "to live is Christ"—when he carried around *another* list of things to live for, a spiel of accolades of accomplishments that validated his relationship with God:

• "Circumcised the eighth day."
• "Of the nation of Israel."

- "Of the tribe of Benjamin."
- "A Hebrew born of Hebrews."
- "As to the law, a Pharisee."
- "As to zeal, persecuting the church."
- "As to the righteousness that is in the law, blameless."

Paul's priorities used to be performance. He considered it his duty to beat people into compliance, thinking all the while that he was on a mission from heaven, that he was doing God a big favor.

But when Christ becomes your life (your *only* life) . . . when Christ becomes your attitude (your *only* attitude), then Christ can become your goal (your *only* goal), just as He did for Paul.

He wrote, "Everything that was a gain to me, I have considered to be a loss because of Christ" (Phil. 3:7). No longer was pedigree, position, or power important to who Paul was or what he wanted to do. Everything changed when he learned he could live without the law.

"More than that, I also consider everything to be a loss in view of the surpassing value of knowing Christ Jesus my Lord" (v. 8). There's that word again—"knowing"—not just possessing a fact or definition in his head but "knowing" by experience that Christ is everything. Jesus was all he needed, all he could ever hope for.

Knowing Jesus. That was his goal. Not knowing how to observe the Sabbath. Not knowing the proper way to walk and talk and look and appear. Not having a "righteousness of my own from the law, but one that is through faith in Christ—the righteousness from God based on faith" (v. 9).

Paul's goal was simply to "know Him" (v. 10), not to knock Him over everyone else's head.

Goalkeeper

What a difference there is between wanting Christ and wanting recognition, between needing Him and needing approval, between *receiving* righteousness and *striving* for righteousness. What a difference between loving our Christian feelings, loving our Christian reputation, loving all the familiar trappings of Christianity . . . and simply loving Christ.

It's never by seeking to know Christ that we become frustrated with our faith. The reason we hit the wall in our Christian life is because we've veered off onto another path—the long, endless road of achievement, accomplishment, and earning our way into God's good graces. When we start adding goal on top of goal on top of goal—the way the "dogs" of Philippi drew it up—our tongues will be hanging out from now till doomsday, trying to get God's attention and special-order His response.

But Paul had one goal: knowing Jesus.

"Not that I have already obtained it or have already become perfect, but I press on so that I may lay hold of that for which also I was laid hold of by Christ Jesus. . . . I press on toward the goal for the prize of the upward call of God in Christ Jesus" (vv. 12, 14 NASB).

You can try to do it your way . . . and fail every time. Or you can surrender your whole life—now and forever—into the loving and capable hands of God.

Sure, you'll still produce works of obedience. You'll be going and serving and loving and embracing. But not because *you're* doing it, not because you're frantically trying to please God and impress your friends. It'll be Christ living in you, changing your life, changing your attitude . . .

Changing your priorities to match His.

Christ Is My Strength: Philippians 4

I like to approach the Bible as if it's a big luggage compartment, with each chapter being its own bag with its own handle. That way, once I understand the main theme of each chapter in a particular book of the Bible, I can get a better grasp on the whole thing, as well as its individual pieces.

Not only that, but when I hear someone teaching on a particular Bible book or throwing around a passage of Scripture, these handles help me tell if he's lifting the verse out of context or if he's taking the big picture into account.

Philippians is an easy book to look at this way—like a luggage rack with four suitcases in it, four handles.

The handle on chapter 1 is the Christian's life.

The handle on chapter 2 is the Christian's attitude.

The handle on chapter 3 is the Christian's goal.

And the handle on chapter 4 is the Christian's strength.

Isn't that what we need? Strength? Isn't that what we know we're lacking when we come up against circumstances that threaten to take our breath away and leave us in a puddle of pity and excuses?

David once captured it this way, crying out to the Lord: "I call to You from the ends of the earth when my heart is without strength. Lead me to a rock that is high above me" (Ps. 61:2). I love that!

Paul was in prison. Never forget that fact when you read Philippians. All these great memory verses from this book that people love so much, all these towering statements of confidence and rejoicing that have inspired God's people through the centuries—they weren't

written while Paul was kicked back on a beach somewhere, celebrating his soul-winning success and counting the income from his cassette tape ministry.

Paul was in a dump . . . but he wasn't in the dumps,
because Christ was his life and Christ was his strength.

That's why I can tell you with absolute assurance
that every one of your life's problems can fit inside this
famous verse—Philippians 4:13: "I am able to do all
things through Him who strengthens me." I can promise
it because I know where Paul was when he wrote it. And
if it worked for him in his prison, it can work for you in
yours.

Inside Information

Some people misapply this passage. They clamp on
to the first half of the verse—the "able to do all things"
part—and act like the back half is just optional information. Sure enough, when Paul said in Philippians 4,
verse 11 that he had "learned to be content in whatever
circumstances I am," the word translated *content*
comes from two words meaning "to suffice himself," to
be self-sufficient.

But this is not the same kind of self-sufficiency that
leads people to think they've got what it takes to overcome life's challenges. This is not the rallying cry we hear
so often about "believing in yourself."

That's why it's so important to know where you are
in the Bible when you're reading and studying it. Yes,
Paul could say he was "content"—self-sufficient—in
every circumstance but only because (as we've been discovering all throughout Philippians) *Paul knew what
was inside himself.* Christ was his life. It wasn't Paul's
guts and gumption that enabled him to thrive inside a

prison cell. It wasn't his inner fortitude that helped him see "progress" being made while chained to a Roman jailer.

The one who lived in Paul was the one who made him able to "do all things." This comprehensive power to knock the top out of any trial was only available "through Him" who gave Paul strength.

And this same Jesus who sat with Paul in prison, who encouraged him in confinement, who taught him "the secret [of being content]—whether well-fed or hungry, whether in abundance or in need" (v. 12), is the same Jesus who lives inside you. Because of Him—because He is now your *life,* your *attitude,* your *goal,* and your *strength*—pleasant circumstances are no longer conditions for your contentment.

When Christ is your life, everything else is just building material.

Ending Up

Has living for Christ become impossible for you? Does it seem as though your current situation has separated you from the source of your strength? Have you run out of energy trying to keep up with the list-takers and guilt-manipulators in your church or in your circle of family and friends?

You'll never find peace on the treadmill of accomplishment. There are too many options, too many questions, too many coaches, and too many opportunities for failure.

But if Paul could look around at his bare-wall situation, if he could throw off the chains of works-based acceptance that had been his love and passion for the better part his life, so can we. So can you.

No, you can never live the Christian life, not as long as it means doing things for God. The futility you feel from taking that tack is genuine. It's shared by millions of others just like yourself who have been there, done that, and now have the red-eye pictures to prove it.

But I invite you today to surrender. To come down from the high-wire act you've been putting on for God's approval. To wad up all the charts and schedules and expectations and do-lists that have kept you running like a rabbit but still feeling like a failure.

Christ is your life. He already loves you. He's already accepted you. He's already died to forgive your sins, free you from the law, and promise you eternity. He already knows what He wants to accomplish through you. He's already put you in the places and around the people where He can live His life through you in perfect accordance with His will.

I'm not saying that you should quit and do nothing. I'm saying, like Paul did, that it's time to let God do the driving. And all you need to do is show up.

Your ride, and your life, is waiting right inside.

CHAPTER 2

Biscuits for Jesus

[All the Goodness,
Baked Right In]

Not too long ago I was on a flight from Switzerland to Johannesburg, South Africa. Seventeen and a half hours. Sitting down. Nothing to do. Sure to be a lot of fun, right?

But shortly after I'd taken my seat, an attractive, energetic young woman plopped down next to me. She had just swung a big business deal of some kind (she later told me), but I could tell right away that she had already celebrated by going shopping. Packages were everywhere.

Still flushed and full of herself from the excitement of her spending spree, she turned to me just as we were taking off, and asked, "What do you do?"

"I'm a preacher," I replied. "I'm going to South Africa to train pastors who live in the bush country."

"Well," she said, "I want you to know something straight out." She was setting the parameters of our conversation from the get-go, making sure I clearly understood the ground rules. "We're going to be on this plane a long time together, so let me tell you right now: *religion has never worked for me.*"

"Thank God," I said, "because it's never worked for me either."

I wish you could have seen the look on her face. "What?" she blurted out.

And long after my computer battery had died, long after I'd read everything in sight, long after I'd seen all the in-flight movies, we continued to talk, off and on, about God and about grace. "Christianity's not a religion," I told her. "It's a relationship."

As we got ready to land, she said to me, "I still have some things in my life I don't want to turn loose of. But I've never heard before what you've been telling me today. I was always taught to do, to do, to do. But I couldn't. And I can't. So I threw it all away."

I hope and pray the Lord has helped her see that it wasn't God who belonged in the garbage; it was everything else.

Have you ever felt the way this young woman did? Have you caught yourself living as though Christianity was a religion instead of a relationship? Do you know what it's like to be constantly sweating under a performance mentality? Do you wish more than anything, though, that you could let the enabling power of God's grace live and flow and work through you?

We looked at this in the last chapter through the lens of Paul's life and experience. But you may be wondering, *Where's the doctrine behind all this?* I mean, it *sounds* great. It *feels* good. But where does Paul document this message of grace?

For that we need to go to Romans 6, one of the most powerful chapters in all the Bible. This is where we learn most clearly . . .

• Our Christian life is not up to us; it's up to Christ.
• We're not demanded to perform but to surrender.
• It's not about being *com*mitted but *sub*mitted.

Homegrown Righteousness

The heart of Romans 6 is verse 14: "For sin will not rule over you, because you are not under law but under grace."

To be "under" something means to be under its "controlling power." Paul used the word *under* several times in the Book of Romans. For example, he described how he was "under obligation" to all men as a minister of the gospel (1:14 NASB). He explained the condition of fallen humanity as being "under sin" (3:9), under its control.

But that's not all. Before we came to know Christ, we were also "under law." We were left to ourselves to accomplish the Ten Commandments and all the other things God had ordered us to do in the Bible. The law stood over us; we stood under it. And it condemned our every effort to achieve what it demanded.

This is the current condition of your unsaved friends and family. Remember that.

But when you received Christ, something radical happened to this arrangement. As Paul said, "No condemnation now exists for those in Christ Jesus, because the Spirit's law of life in Christ Jesus has set you free from the law of sin and of death" (Rom. 8:1–2). One of the most important things God did for us at salvation was to strip away all the demands of the law. His grace, in wiping out our guilt, took the law right along with it.

That's good.

But let me tell you what usually happens next. Almost without our realizing it, the law sneaks back in. It doesn't ask us to do bad things. That's what's so sneaky about it. It encourages us to do *good* things. Religious things. Spiritual-sounding things.

We even do it to other people. I know as a pastor— even though I did it unintentionally—I've put my own church members up under a performance mentality. I'd say to someone, "If you don't do this, if you don't do that, you're not spiritual, you're not doing what God wants." I've probably made a lot of people miserable, including myself, thinking I was doing us all a big favor.

I'm sure you, too, have felt that same kind of pressure. You've thought that in order to be a good Christian, you need to be reading these particular books, praying so many hours a day, handing out a certain number of gospel tracts, and holding down a few more jobs at church. Surely with all of that going for you, God wouldn't have any choice but to look down favorably on you.

Stay with me, now, because this is so critical. The distinctions here can be razor thin. But they are the difference between constant frustration and complete freedom in Christ.

The law wants us to perform righteous acts, good deeds. Whenever you see the term *righteousness* in Scripture, it always means what a person does. Yes, it's also what we *are* as believers—we are the "righteousness of God" (2 Cor. 5:21)—but only because of what Christ has *done*. "Good works" and "righteousness" are synonyms. They are always linked to someone's performance.

God, though, sees our good works in a much different way than we do—not just *before* we're saved but also *after* we're saved. "All of us," Isaiah the prophet wrote, "have become like something unclean, and all our righteous acts are like a polluted garment" (Isa. 64:6). The King James Version calls them "filthy rags."

Imagine that! The way we had it figured, God was supposed to be really impressed by all our praying and fasting and giving and going and doing. How shocking to realize that even our best deeds look like something He'd hold between as little of His thumb and forefinger as possible, holding His nose with the other hand while dropping the whole thing in the trash. Instead of being a sweet-smelling sacrifice, our homemade righteousness hits Him with all the disgusting displeasure of a smelly garbage bag.

Haven't we learned yet, through many long years of trying, that the law cannot produce in us what it demands? That's because those of us who are told to obey it suffer from a chronic weakness of the flesh. Our human nature is simply incapable of producing righteousness. We just can't do it! Not only does it make no sense to try; it stinks to high heaven when we do.

So here's the disconnect: Most of us are pretty clear on the fact that good works can never get a person to heaven. No misunderstanding there. But once we become saved through faith in Christ, through receiving His righteousness, it's not uncommon for us to try performing again as believers.

It's true. Many of us have thrown off the law, only to put ourselves right back up under it again.

Which Comes First?

This was the problem the Galatians had. Paul wrote to them and said, "I only want to learn this from you: Did you receive the Spirit by the works of the law or by hearing with faith? Are you so foolish? After beginning with the Spirit, are you now going to be made complete by the flesh?" (Gal. 3:2–3).

(The Book of Galatians, by the way, is Paul writing Romans mad. Both of these letters have the same message. But what took Paul sixteen chapters to say in Romans took him only six in Galatians. When you're fed up with somebody, you don't waste a lot of words getting to the point.)

The message Paul was trying to get across to both the Galatians and the Romans is one we must never forget: *Jesus has already met all the requirements of the law*—all the righteous standards we were never able to meet before and still aren't able to meet now. And here's why He did it: "In order that the law's requirement would be accomplished in us who do not walk according to the flesh but according to the Spirit" (Rom. 8:4).

There's the difference! It's not what we do for God through our flesh that counts; it's what God does through us by His Spirit.

In Ephesians 2:10, Paul wrote, "For we are His creation—created in Christ Jesus for good works, which

God prepared ahead of time so that we should walk in them."

God has already planned "ahead of time" what He wants to do through us. The good deeds that flow out of our lives are not the things we think up and then ask God to bless. They come instead out of an intimate relationship with the Father, a day-by-day renewing of our minds through His Word—relating to Him, not being religious for Him.

Think back to that well-known verse that says, "All Scripture is inspired by God and is profitable for teaching, for rebuking, for correcting, for training in righteousness" (2 Tim. 3:16). We usually stop it right there, as though the Bible and real life are only casually related. But watch how the next verse completes the sentence: "so that the man of God may be complete, equipped for every good work" (v. 17).

Look at verse 16 again:

• God's "teaching" shows us the track we need to be running on.

• His "rebuking" and "correcting" get us *back* on track when we've fallen off.

• Then His "training" comes along to *keep* us on the right track, reminding us over and over again that our "righteousness" comes from Him and flows through us.

So which comes first? Is it the work? Or is it the Word?

If you want to walk in a continuous stream of God-honoring good works, you'd better be ready to step out from under the law and come up under the Word of God. I'm telling you, when you relate to God through grace, you'll discover something the law can never deliver, no matter how many checks you write, no matter how many pies you bake, no matter how many classes you attend.

And that thing is . . . rest.

How many times has your Christian life felt restful and refreshing to you? When was the last time you entered the day spiritually awake and alive, energized and ready to go?

A person who's at rest isn't lazy and lethargic. No, no. He's simply calm. He's at peace. He's not worried or flustered or spun up. He's aware that he's in good hands. He's assured of God's safety and protection. "For the person who has entered [God's] rest has rested from . . ." From what? Get ready now. He has "rested from his own works, just as God did from His" (Heb. 4:10).

This is not passivity. Just because God has rested from His works, does this mean He's doing absolutely nothing now? Of course not.

It's the same with us. This is not sitting under a tree somewhere, telling God to go get 'em while we go fishing. Relating to God is a *200 percent* relationship. It's God doing it all 100 percent—while we remain 100 percent surrendered to Him in full cooperation with His Word.

On the outside, yes, walking "according to the Spirit" may result in many of the same kinds of things we used to dream up and gut out for God "according to the flesh":

• Bible study
• Prayer
• Giving
• Serving

But be assured, you'll know the difference when it's Him doing it through you instead of you trying to impress

Him. You'll sense the freshness. You'll find yourself bearing Christian qualities like "love, joy, peace, patience, kindness, goodness, faith, gentleness, self-control"—all in abundance. You know why? Because Christ in us is all these things and more. When He lives His life in and through the believer, everyone sees the difference.

And "against such things there is no law" (Gal. 5:22–23).

Double Jeopardy

Our flesh only knows two ways of responding to the law:

• One is *rebellion*.
• The other is *religion*.

Put me under a diet, and I'll tell you how my flesh will react. Rebelliously. Put us under a speed limit, and most of us will push it as far as we can go without getting caught.

But start a new exercise routine, and see how many ways you find to work your progress into an average conversation. Whatever the flesh doesn't rebel against, it revels in.

Jesus' parable of the prodigal son painted this picture perfectly. The younger son, of course—the prodigal—rebelled against the restrictions of living at home, running away with his inheritance and blowing every penny of it on "loose living." Back home, though, his older brother reacted no less sinfully, only differently, priding himself in the way he'd been keeping the house rules over the years. One was rebellious; the other was religious.

You see the same thing in the first few chapters of Romans. The second half of chapter 1—the passage that talks about how "God delivered them over" to their degrading pursuits—speaks of the rampant "evil, greed, and wickedness" (v. 24) and everything else that occurs when people know what God wants but refuse to submit to it. Chapter 2 and most of chapter 3, however, describe what happens when people "rest in the law, and boast in God" (2:17), looking down their pious noses at those who don't measure up.

Two reactions. Both sinful. This is all our flesh knows to do.

So when you come to a law in Scripture, remember . . . you're not "under law." God doesn't expect you to perform that. You're "under grace." He expects you only to surrender to Him, so He can perform it through you.

See the difference?

When the Scripture teaches you to love people you don't like, God says, *You can't do that.* But when you realize that He is more than able to love that person through you, guess what? He'll produce in you what you don't have the ability to produce within yourself.

When the Scripture instructs you about the importance of spending time in prayer, you'll be tempted to think, *I can attain that. I can do that.* No, you can't! As long as you approach God in your flesh, all you'll end up doing is making yourself feel spiritually snobby and superior. But if you'll release all the responsibility to Christ, He'll create in you a hunger for Him that could never be ignited by your own wants and willpower.

Performance. The law demands it, but it cannot produce it. The only one who's capable of doing it is the one who's already fulfilled the law, the Spirit of Christ who dwells in us, who lives "inside the coat." He does through us what we cannot do ourselves.

Perhaps this will help make it even plainer: Christ comes to live in us so that He can do His work through us . . . with no help from us!

And Now . . . Back to Romans

All of the things we've been talking about in this chapter—our "filthy rags" pursuit of righteousness, our tendency to put good works ahead of the Word of God, our two inevitable reactions to living "under the law"— take us back to where we started. Each of us knows how many times we've fallen victim to all three of these harsh realities. As a result, not only have we failed to justify ourselves before God; we've also allowed "sin" to "rule" over us (Rom. 6:14).

Yuck. What a mess!

So let's trail back through this important sixth chapter of Romans to see how Paul got to verse 14—and to see what we can do to get there ourselves.

Verses 1–5: Getting Us Energized

The first thing you discover when you're "under grace" is that you're a brand-new person in Christ. The legalists, of course, have a hard time digesting this. It's just too easy. They hate to think that someone less holier-than-thou could somehow be considered equal with them before God.

But Paul also had another bunch of listeners who were twisting his grace message in the other direction. These were the antinomians—a name that comes from the prefix *anti* (meaning "against") and *nomos* (meaning "law"). Unlike the legalists these people mistook God's grace, thinking it gave them free license to do whatever they wanted. They didn't realize (or didn't *want* to realize) that freedom doesn't mean the right to do as we please but rather the power to do as we should.

"What should we say then?" Paul asked them. "Should we continue in sin in order that grace may multiply? Absolutely not! How can we who died to sin still live in it?" (Rom. 6:1–2).

They wanted life without death. They wanted the guilt-free enjoyment of their own weaknesses rather than the God-given privilege of being "strong" in his "grace" (2 Tim. 2:1). But death must always come first. This is so important. As Jesus had said earlier, "Unless a grain of wheat falls into the ground and dies, it remains by itself. But if it dies, it produces a large crop" (John 12:24).

So Paul wrote, "Are you unaware that all of us who have been baptized into Christ Jesus were baptized into His death?" (Roms. 6:3). This means that we have been both *immersed* in Him as well as *identified* with Him.

Let me go at it this way: If you sink a white cloth into a bowl of red dye, that cloth is now immersed. Baptism is a living picture of this. We are "buried with Him by baptism into death" (v. 4). But when the cloth is raised up out of the bowl, it is also visibly marked or identified by its contact with the dye. It's not a *white* cloth anymore; it's a *red* cloth, something different than it was before. We are (as Jesus was) "raised from the dead by the glory of the Father, so we too may walk in a new way of life" (v. 4).

Two different Greek words can be translated "new." One of them is what we mean when we say, "I've got a new car." It's the word *neos*. Sure, the car is new but only because it's replacing the one we had before. It's a new car, a different car, but it's still just another car, another version of the same thing.

The second word, though, is *kainos,* which means "absolutely, qualitatively brand-new." For example, if instead of telling you I'd gotten a new car, I told you I went and bought a new *spaceship,* you'd know I wasn't talking about a trade-in but a totally new kind of machine, something we've never had in our driveway before—ever!

That's the word used here to express "a new way of life." Because our old man has been put to death in Christ, He has created a brand-new person in us who never existed before.

Therefore, Paul went on to say—like a lawyer laying out his case before a jury—"if we have been joined with Him in the likeness of His death, we will certainly also be in the likeness of His resurrection" (v. 5).

This is starting to get good now!

Just like before, there are two Greek words that convey the idea of "with," which is the key piece of verse 5. One of these words (*meta*) means the "with" of association. When you're in church on Sunday, you're "with" a group of people. But once the service is over, you'll all hop in your cars and head in different directions. You were "with" one another for a little while, but you always had the ability to leave, to separate from one another. That's *meta.*

The word used in verse 5, however, is not *meta* but *sun,* which can be pronounced "soon" or "seen." This is the "with" of intimacy—a "with" that is inseparable.

I like to think of it in terms of biscuits. Not little wimpy biscuits. Not whomped-on-the-counter biscuits. I'm talking about big old cat-head biscuits. You with me?

Now when people get ready to make a batch of cat-head biscuits, they get out their flour, their baking soda, their salt, and whatever else goes in there. As long as all these ingredients are sitting in their little containers on the counter, they're arranged in the *meta* position. They are "with" one another by association.

But as soon as they're mixed in to the dough and baked in the oven, a molecular change occurs in the whole chemistry of each biscuit. What were once stand-alone ingredients can no longer be taken out and sorted back into the piles they came from. They are now "with" one another in a *sun* kind of relationship. Nobody can ever separate them again from the finished product.

We are biscuits for Jesus. Christ has baked Himself into us so that we are "united" with Him in a unique, grace-filled relationship. We were "with" Him on the cross. We were "with" Him at His resurrection. And we are still "with" Him now, as He lives in us and enables us to be everything He wants us to be.

Verses 6–11: Getting Sin Neutralized

So far, so good.

But not so fast, because let's be honest—even though God has done all these marvelous things to create us into new and righteous people, we don't always act new and righteous. It doesn't take us long as believers to realize that even though we're saved, we've got a new kind of struggle on our hands. We may have quit chasing after sin, but watch out—sin has started chasing after us!

And trying to fight it by doing better—by obeying the law—just makes things worse.

That's because the only part of us that's in gear when we try to manufacture our own righteousness is our flesh, our "old self," the person we used to be before we were saved. This is the same person who was never able to please God before and hasn't discovered how to do it since.

Thank God, then, for the encouraging reality check in Romans 6:6: "We know that our old self was crucified with Him in order that sin's dominion over the body may be abolished, so that we may no longer be enslaved to sin."

This tells us a lot about sin's power. First of all, it alerts us to something we've always suspected but hated to admit: we still have a "body" of sin. We wake up with it every morning.

And second, it teaches us that we can't just shift our "old self" into drive and mow down the sins that continually clobber us and drag us away.

Here's why: The word translated "abolished" or "done away with" in this verse is *katargeo* (from *kata,* meaning "down," and *argeo,* meaning "to be idle"). This indicates that for the time being, sin's power has been disengaged in our lives. It's still there, but it's like a car that's idling. It's been thrown into neutral by the strong arms of almighty God.

Can we still hop in and drive it? You bet. There's nothing keeping us from reengaging our lusts and putting them into gear. And every time we do, sin will ignite with the fuel of our flesh, and we will find ourselves behind an all too familiar wheel—the vicious cycle of sin's destruction.

It may show itself through obvious moral failure, the way a car will snap a fan belt. Or it may show itself through our prideful enjoyment of the bells and whistles that separate us from the other riffraff on the road.

But whether through rebellion or religion, any of our efforts at occupying the driver's seat will always result in revving up a "body of sin" that God has already geared down. Any movement to defeat it on our part will do nothing more than stir it up.

Our only defense against sin in this life is total surrender—not trying to walk *over* it, not trying to walk *around* it, but "as you have received Christ Jesus the Lord, walk *in Him*" (Col. 2:6). The same way we entered into salvation—by bowing, submitting, trusting, believing—is the same way we experience victory over sin, day by day. "A person who has died is freed from sin's claims" (Rom. 6:7).

This is so key. This is what God means when he talks about "renewing" our minds (Rom. 12:2), letting His Word saturate our thinking and believing. The more we understand, meditate, and dwell on the awesome reality that we have been "freed" from sin—declared pure and righteous through the saving work of Christ—the more we will see God making it happen in real, tangible ways in our lives. I guarantee it.

This is no mental trick or sleight of hand. This is choosing to walk in truth, to walk in Christ.

Yes, we are always going to be lured toward sin. We will always have a tendency to rebel. Don't even pretend this isn't true. Our flesh has not been eradicated. But the beautiful thing is, God has put a prejudiced will within us. His spirit in us has far more power than our flesh does.

We tend to believe the opposite. We think our sin nature is too big to be manhandled. But that's because we've been focusing on how powerful our sin is rather than how powerful our God is. "He has rescued us from the domain of darkness and transferred us into the kingdom of the Son He loves" (Col. 1:13).

The word for "rescued" in this verse means not only to be delivered from the *presence* of something but also from its *power*. And the "domain" we've been rescued from is both the right and the might of sin's "darkness."

This reminds me of a time when I was thrown from my canoe while riding white water down the San Marcos River in Texas. The life jacket I was wearing wasn't really big enough for a person my size (six foot seven), so I was barely able to keep myself afloat.

Hypothermia quickly began to set in, the water around me being something like forty degrees. Pretty soon I couldn't even raise my arms. I couldn't fight back. I couldn't do *anything*. I was at the total mercy of the stream, which was pulling me down with every rip of current.

All I could do was cry for help.

Thank the Lord, He finally worked me closer to the bank where I could grab an overhanging branch and eventually roll my way clear of the water. So in the hour that passed before someone was able to find me, I lay there—rescued not from the *presence* but from the *power* of the river. Its swirling rapids were still roaring in my ears, but its power could no longer reach me.

Every one of us was born in the current of sin, being carried along toward the pits of hell to be separated from God forever. All we could do was cry out for help. But as David put it, "He reached down from on high and took hold of me; He pulled me out of deep waters" (Ps. 18:16).

Yes, sin is still present, but we've been delivered from its power. Our only job now is to submit and surrender, not to stop at simply *being* under grace but actually *living* under grace.

Maybe one of the subtle reasons we stumble in this area is because, while we're so intimately familiar with Christ's death on the cross—and grateful for the forgiveness He won for us there—we tend to minimize what He did for us through His resurrection.

Please, now, don't hear me downplaying Christ's crucifixion. Without His death, without the mercy that flowed through His blood and into our guilty hearts, we would all be hopelessly lost with nowhere to turn for help.

But look at the focus of Romans 6: 8–10: "Now if we died with Christ, we believe that we will also live with Him, because we know that Christ, having been raised from the dead, no longer dies. Death no longer rules over Him. For in that He died, He died to sin once for all; but in that He lives, He lives to God."

See what I'm talking about? His death—thank God—saved us from the *penalty* of sin. But His life is what continually saves us from the *power* of sin. His death made our life with Him possible. But His life in us is what makes today livable. "For if, while we were enemies, we were reconciled to God through the death of His Son, [then how] much more, having been reconciled, will we be saved by His life!" (Rom. 5:10).

Verses 12–14: Getting Unlegalized

The truth, then, is that God has rescued us from sin. Yet for some reason known only to His surpassing wisdom and sovereignty, He has left sin hanging around for us to choose it if we want it.

And choose it, we often do.

I'm afraid, though, we give the devil way too much credit for his role in this sin battle of ours. It's hard to get away from those convicting words in James 1:14–15 that say, "Each person is tempted when he is drawn away and enticed by his own evil desires. Then after desire has conceived, it gives birth to sin."

I hate to admit it. I really do. But—being real honest here—I can't think of a better way to describe my own experience with sin and temptation than this passage from James does. These words just nail me cold. I could wish I had someone else to blame for it, but I know differently.

When it comes to sin, I do it to myself.

Paul seemed to be following in the same vein when he said, "Therefore do not let sin reign in your mortal body, so that you obey its desires" (Rom. 6:12). These "desires" or "lusts" he talked about are better described by the Greek word he actually used: *epithumia.* The *thumia* part means "passion," and *epi* is sort of an intensifier. In a biblical sense they are any fleshly itches we want scratched so badly we'll sin to get them.

I know mine. You know yours.

And the only way—*the only way*—to make sure you keep these lusts under control is to "not go on presenting the members of your body to sin as instruments of unrighteousness; but present yourselves to God as those alive from the dead, and your members as instruments of righteousness to God" (v. 13 NASB).

I know that's a mouthful, but don't miss the message. In fact, take just a second to read verse 13 again . . . and again, if necessary, until this truth comes through: We don't overcome sin by working ourselves to death trying *not* to do bad things. We overcome sin by offering ourselves to God.

It's not what we turn away from; it's who we turn to.

These Roman readers Paul was writing to were a lot like we are. The passage of two thousand years doesn't change a lot in terms of who people are on the inside and how we relate to God. The Roman believers were regularly "presenting" their bodies to sin. Their sexual appetites, their desire for reputation, their greed for money, power, and things. All of these "lusts" had an active-tense position in their lives.

But Paul admonished them not to keep on "presenting" these lusts as fodder for unrighteousness. The word itself that's translated "presenting" in this verse is *paristemi,* which means "to place beside." Paul was basically telling the believers in Rome not to go *near* sin and temptation, to stay as far away from "unrighteousness" as they could possibly get.

But the second part of this verse is critical to our understanding. The opposite of being sinful is not just avoiding sin. The opposite of being sinful is submitting to Christ, letting him produce his righteousness in us.

Try to remember it this way: *Victory in the Christian life is not you overcoming sin; it's Jesus overcoming you.*

"For sin will not rule over you, because you are not under law but under grace" (v. 14). As long as the law is your master, sin will be your master too. But when your only Master is Christ, sin has no choice but to take a back seat.

This certainly doesn't mean we'll handle things perfectly every time. But the greatest freedom comes from just being honest. When our flesh gets out of bounds on us—and it will—the key is not to let it camp out there. Just immediately shift gears and put your focus back on Christ. Let His truth and forgiveness flow back in.

You have already been "declared righteous" or "justified by faith" (Rom. 5:1). This means the same thing as being *acquitted*—your slate wiped clean, your record expunged. All the sin and guilt in your life was erased when you believed in Christ, when He lifted the demands of the law from your shoulders.

As a result, "we have peace with God through our Lord Jesus Christ" (Rom. 5:1). We've dropped our sword. We're not fighting Him anymore. Therefore, whatever His Word teaches us to do, our answer is *yes*. Whatever his Spirit leads us to do, our answer is *yes*.

Just . . . *yes!* That's the new theme that grows out of this "not under law but under grace" mentality.

Christ has done something glorious for us in our past. He has "obtained" for us "access by faith into this grace in which we stand" (Rom. 5:2). This is a fixed state of being. Even on days when we're not being very faithful, Christ continues to be faithful in us because we eternally "stand" in His grace.

We are no longer "under the law." Therefore, sin can never again claim the right to "rule" over us, unless we want it to.

Why, then, do we ever choose to put ourselves back up under law? Why do we ever think performing for Jesus is better than letting Him live His life through us? Why do we shackle ourselves down again, grinding out our obedience as though it was all up to us, chaining ourselves to self-prescribed regimens of Christian discipline and drudgery?

Again, I'm not saying for one minute that we should let ourselves become lazy, spiritual slobs. Oh, let me tell you, people will accuse you of this if you adopt a lifestyle of grace. They'll come down on you from now till suppertime for not pulling your weight and not doing enough of the right things—*their* things.

But I've walked that double-duty road enough times to know: its only destination is misery. There's nothing the least bit attractive about a Christian life that's bound up by law, measures, and customs.

Remember: *I can't—God never said I could. He can—and He always said He would.*

When you experience God's living grace, you'll not only be able to enjoy and celebrate your permanent status—as being righteous before God—but you'll also experience the joy of watching Him live out His righteousness in you.

Makes me hungry for biscuits. How about you?

CHAPTER 3

Legally Dead

[The Frustration of Living under Law]

I love that *Andy Griffith Show* episode where Barney Fife is coming out of church, after sleeping through most of the sermon, and says to the preacher, "Yes, sir, that's one thing you can't talk about enough—sin."

Ol' Barn may have had the subject of the message wrong. But he was certainly right about our usual response to hard-line sermons on the big, bad sins— the kind of sins that land people in scandal and disgrace, the kind that give us (like the Pharisee in Jesus' parable) an excuse to be glad that we're "not like other people" (Luke 18:11).

Oh, yes, we are.

One of the main things we need to get through our heads if we're ever to understand God's message of grace is this: the sin of being *religious* is every bit as bad as the sin of being *rebellious*.

I know this is not the way most of us were conditioned. We tend to prefer the cut-and-dried, step-by-step formula, the personal achievement of doing things ourselves. We like the praise and applause we receive for our efforts in righteousness. We've wished, in fact, for *more*—more compliments, more congratulations, more kind words to be said about us . . . where everybody can hear them.

No doubt, living under the law can pay out some nice, short-term dividends every now and then.

But if we really want the law, if we really want to live under its strict demands and expectations, we'd better know what we're dealing with. "For whoever keeps the entire law, yet falls in one point, is guilty of [breaking it] all" (James 2:10).

Add to this the fact that the law condemns not only our human *rebellion* but also our human *righteousness* . . . and this can be a recipe for real frustration.

Smashing Results

You've probably heard the story about the two hunters who came across a huge hole one day while they were out in the woods together. It was the biggest, deepest hole they'd ever seen. In fact, it didn't even appear to have a bottom to it!

So just for fun, they threw a small rock into the hole to see how long it would take before it hit. Hearing nothing, they tried bigger rocks, then bigger rocks—even one that took both of them to carry.

But every time, no sound. Nothing.

Finally, they grabbed both ends of a loose railroad tie that was lying nearby, heaving it over the edge and into the hole. It hurtled end-over-end into the blackness. But still, they couldn't detect any sound to indicate how deep the bottom was.

Then suddenly—scrambling out of the bushes—a lone goat came flying at a dead sprint, shot right between the two of them, sailed headlong into the hole, and was gone!

Just as they were starting to get their wits back together, the old farmer who owned the place wheeled his pickup into the clearing. The two hunters motioned for him to spool down his window, then said, "Hey, you won't believe what just happened! A goat came sailing through those trees and ran straight into this big hole here. Was he yours?"

"No, couldn't be," the farmer drawled. "My goat was staked out to a railroad tie."

(Stay with it, now. It gets funnier the more you think about it.)

But Christians who insist on staying attached to the law—like the goat was to the railroad beam—are destined to face the same thing: a sure dead end, the absolute certainty of repeated, rock-bottom failure. There's simply no other way.

Oh, we can pretend that our performance is getting results. We can convince ourselves that we're impressing God and putting everybody else to shame. But are we really? If we were truly honest with ourselves, wouldn't we have to admit that we're probably not fooling anybody?

Being honest with ourselves, though, doesn't tend to come naturally to us, does it?

Good thing, though, that the Bible knows a lot about being honest.

So when we're ready ourselves to start getting incredibly honest with God about our affinity for the law, a good place to begin is the seventh chapter of Romans because in this key passage of Scripture, we discover:

- How the law feeds our sin.
- How sin then begins to eat away at us.
- But how Jesus (if we'll let Him) really satisfies.

You want the law? Well, let's give Paul a chance to expose the law for what it really is . . . and then see how much you like it.

Verses 1–6: The Principle of Law

Paul was a master at logical argument. For years, in fact, law schools used the Book of Romans to show students how to construct their cases. Each of Paul's points, inspired (of course) by the Holy Spirit, was carefully built upon the other—piece by piece—until he had painted the legalists into such a corner, the only way they could look more foolish was by insisting they liked it there.

His first appeal in chapter 7 was to *common knowledge*—to man's familiarity with law. Not *the* law (the definite article *the* doesn't appear in the original text), but simply "law" in general.

We all know what it's like to have laws that govern us. We know what it means, for example, when we spot a state trooper's car parked in the grassy median of the interstate. We know why the election officials want to see our voter's card before we cast a ballot. We know what the folks at the superstore exit door are doing when they ask to look in our bags and check our receipt. The law has a controlling, condemning power over mankind that is merely part of the human experience.

So that was point number one: confirming the law's position as an authority over us.

Paul's next appeal was to *common sense*. "Since I am speaking to those who understand law, brothers, are you unaware that the law has authority over someone as long as he lives?" (Rom. 7:1).

Sure. If the defendant in a criminal case decides to hang himself before his trial is complete, do the lawyers, witnesses, and jury have anything left to convene for? Once the guy is dead, there's little point in sweeping out a jail cell for him, right?

Two pitches from Paul, two strikes on the batter.

Finally, then, just before he drilled his point all the way home, Paul appealed to his readers with a *common example*.

"For example, a married woman is legally bound to her husband while he lives. But if her husband dies, she is released from the law regarding her husband. So then, if she gives herself to another man while her husband is living, she will be called an adulteress. But if her husband dies, she is free from that law. Then, if she gives herself to another man, she is not an adulteress" (vv. 2–3).

How can you argue with this kind of logic? When a woman's husband dies, she will miss him, she will grieve over him, she'll have a hard time going on without him. But one thing's for sure: if she does choose to remarry, she will not be guilty of unfaithfulness. Once her husband is dead, she can't be accused of running around on him.

The reason this whole exercise of verses 1–3 is so important is because God is not asking us to believe something that's wildly irrational.

We understand the concept of law.

We understand the concept of death.

We understand the concept of marriage.

Anyone, then, can grasp the key ingredients of the gospel.

Something Old, Something New

After these three little verses in chapter 7, each of which had been established by the lessons of chapter 6, Paul had his dominoes in place right where he wanted them. So by the time he got to verse 4, he was ready to move from common ground to direct conclusions.

"Therefore, my brothers, you also were put to death in relation to the law through the crucified body of the Messiah, so that you may belong to another" (Rom. 7:4). It's all there: law, death, and marriage—all in one sentence—and all wrapped up in the work of Jesus Christ.

I love the way Paul did this. I mean, he'd set his readers up so well, they couldn't help but see the truth, even if they still felt the need to fuss about it.

1. Yes, there is a law, which stands in authority over the entire human race.

2. But guess what, a death has occurred—Jesus' death—terminating the law's jurisdiction over Him.

3. And so those of us who have been "buried with him," who have been "baptized into his death" (remember Romans 6?) are now free to be united with a new bridegroom—Christ.

Beautiful, isn't it? This is what happened to us at salvation. This is the promise of the good news!

But wait, it gets better! Not only are we in a new relationship with Christ that guarantees us eternal life; we have been joined "to Him who was raised from the dead—that we may bear fruit for God" (v. 4). We have not only been freed from our past; we have also become empowered to do something we could never do before.

"For when we were in the flesh,"—when we were lost—"the sinful passions operated through the law in every part of us and bore fruit for death" (v. 5).

In our previous marriage—our marriage to the law—the only "fruit" we were able to produce, the only children (so to speak) we were able to bear, were those who were destined for "death." So as long as we were bound up in a relationship to the law, death and all of its nasty side effects were the best we could ever hope for.

"But now we have been released from the law, since we have died to what held us, so that we may serve in the new way of the Spirit and not in the old letter of the law" (v. 6). Now that we live under grace—and as long as we refuse to place ourselves back up under law as believers—we're able to "bear fruit for God" as He lives His life through us. This is because, as Paul said, we have been "released from the law."

That word for "released" in verse 6 is the same one we looked at in verse 6 of Romans chapter 6—*katargeo*—which means "to idle down," to place in neutral. The law (just like sin) still exists, but its hold on us has been "released." At one time, yes, we were bound to it, married to it. But "having died" with Christ, having received His salvation, our obligation to the law has been severed. Now we are free to walk in newness rather than oldness—in the "new way" rather than the "old letter."

The whole thing fits like a glove, doesn't it? Paul's argument holds together with no holes for contradiction and no place for misunderstanding. "Old things have passed away, and look, new things have come" (2 Cor. 5:17).

This is the present reality for all of us who are in Christ.

But we have to be careful because although Christ does live within us, pulling us toward the Father, our flesh still has a taste for the old way of life. "And no one, after drinking old wine wishes for new; for he says, 'The old is good enough'" (Luke 5:39 NASB).

Guard your heart against this kind of thinking. The "old"—the law—may show some prideful signs of life from time to time. It may be able to scratch a few of your itches here and there. But every time you've found yourself exposed by your own hypocrisy, every time you've failed to do what you knew you should, every time you've felt cheated because others weren't patting you on the back enough, you've swallowed death back into your heart again. And you know how bad it tastes.

So you tell me, is that old stuff really "good enough" for you?

Or are you dying for something better?

Verses 7–13: The Purpose of Law

Not many people would call Romans 7 one of their favorite chapters in the Bible. Romans 6, maybe—the one that talks about how the "the gift of God is eternal life in Christ Jesus our Lord" (v. 23). Or Romans 8, where we find out "no condemnation now exists for those in Christ Jesus" (v. 1).

But I like Romans 7 best because it helps me understand what makes chapters 6 and 8 so wonderful. Without Romans 7, we can't even *begin* to comprehend the depths of depravity we've been rescued from or be nearly thankful enough for what Christ has won for us.

In this middle stretch of Romans 7, in fact, we even get to see the great apostle Paul coming totally clean about his past and his daily struggles with sin. How encouraging this is to me! Here was a man who had founded church after church, whose Christian friends cherished his every word and wept like babies whenever he left town, admitting in print to the same conflicts we all face on a regular basis.

How could this happen to a man like him and to people like us?

It's because of the twin relationship between sin and the law.

• *The law* represents everything we can never do on our own, every bad thing we can't help avoiding on willpower alone.

• *And sin,* recognizing our inability to perform the law, takes the "opportunity" (v. 8) to launch its assault on us.

That word which is translated as "opportunity" literally means "to build a base camp." Just like when military units invade a hostile country, advancing to a point where they can attack with precision at close proximity, sin camps onto the commandments of the law to exploit our human weaknesses.

So lay down any sin—like coveting, for example (v. 7)—even in front of the disciplined demeanor of an apostle Paul, and what did he do, if left to his own devices? He coveted all day long. He couldn't help it.

It's funny, we tend to think these Bible writers were walking answer books their whole lives, people who knew everything there was to know about following Christ. But I believe (personal opinion here) that this matter about sin's relationship with the law was a truth Paul didn't discover until many years after his Damascus Road experience.

You'll remember in Galatians 1–2, where he recapped his own history, that he talked about an interval of fourteen years or more between the time when he was converted and when his ministry finally began in earnest. I believe this was the period he was referring to when he said, "Once I was alive apart from the law" (Rom. 7:9), during those special years when he was being taught and instructed by the Holy Spirit in the ways of grace. But when he came back to Jerusalem, back around his peers, I think that old religious flesh of his fired back to life.

This must have shocked him to realize that the law still had such a strong pull on his affections, to sense how easy it was—even after all of that time—to step right back into his old, familiar pattern of nit-picking and finger-pointing.

The commandments, you see, had come back—the law had reappeared in his life, with all of its unattainable point totals and tally marks—and look what happened to him:

- "Sin sprang to life" in him (v. 9).
- It resulted in "death for me" (v. 10).
- It "deceived me, . . . it killed me" (v. 11).

Know the feeling?

I sure do.

That's because *the law can never produce in us what it requires.* (Never forget that.) Only through Christ— only through grace—do we escape being pinched between sin and the law, squeezed into a corner with nothing but failure and frustration to keep us company.

There's no other way. Either Christ produces His life-giving fruit within us, or we sprout constant death all day long.

A Top-Ten, No-Win Situation

We do, however, have the law to thank for one thing: were it not for the law, we would never know just how sinful we are.

This may not be a fact you've been dying to know, but it truly is a refreshing taste of reality to those of us who've been killing ourselves covering our tracks, trying like crazy to mask our sinfulness through a lot of spiritual plate spinning.

Our sin stinks bad. Even our sins of self-righteousness! And were it not for the law, we'd have no way of knowing it. We'd be like a person who had no concept of pain, who had no way to grasp the gravity of the danger he was in.

No, the law doesn't cause death, but it reveals what does. That thing is sin. And the closer we get to God, the more awful our sin becomes to us.

Paul, for example, once said he was "the least of the apostles" (1 Cor. 15:9), the worst of the core group who served as Christ's main eyewitnesses. A little later on, he declared that he was "the least of all the saints" (Eph. 3:8), the lowest of all God's people. But nearer the end of his life, Paul saw his flesh in a despicable class all by itself, considering himself to be the "worst," the "chief" of all sinners (1 Tim. 1:16). The longer he lived, the more he realized how sinful he was.

Is this the law's fault? Has the law made us this way? No, "the law is holy, and the commandment is holy and just and good" (Rom. 7:12). There's nothing wrong with the law, but it does bring out something horrible in us.

It makes our sin appear "sinful beyond measure" (v. 13). As the New American Standard puts it, "utterly sinful."

If you want to test the truth of this diagnosis, try waking up tomorrow with a firm resolve to obey the Ten Commandments the rest of this week. Shoot, there's only a few of them—two little handfuls—not the six hundred or more that the Pharisees eventually coded and came up with. So try these on for size:

• Commit yourself to having "no other gods before me," and see how many gods you've been serving without even knowing it.

• Try not to make any "graven image," and discover how many things in your life you're not willing to live without.

• Make a real effort not to take the name of the Lord in vain, and find out how lightly you tend to treat his glory and honor.

• Tell yourself to "remember the sabbath day, to keep it holy," and see what selfish activities and pursuits qualify as top priorities in your life.

• Force yourself to honor your father and your mother, and listen to what your heart says when their instruction goes against your wishes.

• Make plans not to kill someone through your anger, and feel your neck burn the first time someone cuts you off in traffic.

• Promise not to entertain the thought of adultery, and see how long you're able to hang in there before your eyes override your intentions.

• Refuse to steal, and feel the tug of the gray areas, whether it's a borrowed CD you want to copy or an idea you'd like to claim as your own.

• Grit your teeth against bearing false witness, and see what happens when a person you hate being around asks if you have lunch plans.

• Or like Paul, try not to covet, and feel the ache in every jealous bone of your body.

Something will happen. Someone will cross you. Some scheduling conflict will arise. Some appliance will break down. Some unreasonable complaint will come your direction.

And sin will take the "opportunity" to reintroduce you to your flesh. I guarantee it.

So don't gloss over these two words from verse 13 too quickly. *Utterly sinful.* This is what the law has exposed us as being. Our flesh is totally, irreparably evil.

And for the blessing of being shown this, we should thank God because when we realize our utter sinfulness, we're finally in the right place to begin walking under grace.

Verses 14–25: The Problem of Law

Some people, when reading this passage in Romans, conclude that Paul must be talking about what used to happen in his life before he received Christ. They maintain that a saved person wouldn't, shouldn't, or couldn't experience this kind of spiritual difficulty.

They say, for example, "Look at verse 14 in chapter 7. Paul says he is 'of flesh, sold into sin's power.' That *proves* he's an unbeliever!"

Well, there's a big difference between being *of* flesh and being *in* the flesh. When writing to the church in Corinth, Paul labeled the believers there as "people of the flesh" (1 Cor. 3:1). They were saved, of course, but were still operating out of their natural wants and desires—Christians going around "living like ordinary people" in far too many of their attitudes and practices (1 Cor. 3:3).

But this is not the way the Bible describes the unsaved. The lost are not merely *of* flesh but are *in* the flesh. And those who "are *in* the flesh are unable to please God"—at all, ever!—because the Spirit of God doesn't dwell in them (Rom. 8:8–9). Those who are in the flesh are not in Christ.

So thank God that as Christians we are no longer *in* the flesh—no longer under its control. Yet we still have fleshly bodies that are passionately addicted to sin. So every day, we are confronted with the fact that a terrific power for evil and pride still lurks within us.

I mean, come on! Let's get real here.

The good news is, our flesh doesn't get an automatic victory anymore—not the way it used to before we were saved. It no longer has unchecked power to defeat us. *Real* power is in the blood, which covers us from being condemned by the law. *Real* power is in the Holy Spirit, who enables us to rise above the mere keeping of rules and laws, into a pure, Christ-initiated obedience that pleases our heavenly Father.

Just because we are "of flesh" doesn't mean we have no hope. It simply means we have no hope in *ourselves*.

All 100 percent of our hope resides in the risen Christ and, glory to God, we have 100 percent of Christ residing in us.

This is the grace that's available to us on a moment-by-moment basis.

But still, can we look each other in the eye and deny that when we hear Paul's honest description of his inner-man dilemma in Romans 7, of his daily struggle with sin, we all know how hauntingly familiar it sounds?

"For I do not understand what I am doing, because I do not practice what I want to do, but I do what I hate. . . . I do not do the good that I want to do, but I practice the evil that I do not want to do" (vv. 15, 19).

Am I the only one who's had a day like that recently?

"For in my inner self I joyfully agree with God's law. But I see a different law in the parts of my body, waging war against the law of my mind and taking me prisoner to the law of sin in the parts of my body" (vv. 22–23).

These verbs Paul used in this passage are all in the present tense. He was talking about an active experience in his life, being transparent. He was painfully aware that his flesh had a strong tendency to lead him back into his old way of thinking, back when he attempted to please God through his own unending effort, his keeping of the law.

But after seeing again how utterly futile this was, he was forced to admit that "nothing good lives in me" (v. 18). Does this sound like something a lost person would ever say? "The desire to do what is good is with me, but there is no ability to do it" (v. 18). What unsaved person ever felt this way, wanting to love God more completely, wanting to serve Him more faithfully, wanting to be led by His Spirit?

No, Paul's story is our story. It's the story of the Christian life. Every one of us is honestly perplexed that our desire to do better is always being challenged by a flesh that wants its own way, its own credit, and its own glory—contrary to everything we believe and desire in our hearts.

Isn't this what drives us crazy? We love the Lord so much, how can our flesh be such a hater of God and an enemy of the cross? But it is! Every day! As Paul quoted the psalmist, "There is no one righteous, not even one" (Rom. 3:10).

This is indeed a humbling place to reach. It's not pleasant at all to think about. But, oh, the joy and freedom that flows from finally realizing that "if I do what I do not want, I am no longer the one doing it, but it is the sin that lives in me" (Rom. 7:20).

This flesh of ours cannot be patched, improved, or perked up. If our flesh is changing at all, it is only moving in the direction of being more "corrupted by deceitful desires" (Eph. 4:22). It can't be reformed; it must be replaced. We must put on "the new man, the one created according to God's likeness in righteousness and purity of the truth" (v. 24), because our flesh doesn't stand a chance of pulling off anything good on its own.

When I was saved—at age thirty-two, after eight years in Christian ministry (can you believe that?)—this was how Christ got through to me. I had grown up knowing how to play the game, how to mouth the words, how to get by and get the brownie points for it. But when I asked God one morning to show me just how sinful my flesh was, He let me see at least a little of what it looked like to Him.

I wept. I moaned. My nose ran until it bled. But from that day to this, I've never minded anyone telling me that my flesh is sinful. I know it is. I see it in the mirror every morning.

In this, however, I have hope that Christ lives in me, and He alone makes me righteous before the throne.

It is so critical for us to get to this point in our understanding. As I've said before—and will probably say again before I'm through:

I can't—God never said I could.

He can—and He always said He would.

"Therefore we do not give up; even though our outer person is being destroyed, our inner person is being renewed day by day" (2 Cor. 4:16).

Did I Say That?

Several years back, when our kids were still young, we took the family out to Colorado for some spring skiing. It was one of those vacations that was supposed to be so memorable, so unforgettable, but it turned out to be mostly miserable and uncomfortable.

We were from the South, so we had no way of knowing, but even when it's twenty degrees and freezing cold on a Rocky Mountain spring morning, it reaches the seventies by noon. So there we were on our first day out—with all of our layers and our long underwear on, our wool socks and sweaters, our hats and gloves— sweating like mules before we even got up to the slopes.

Not only that, but the whole trip had gotten way more expensive than I thought it would. The lift tickets were high enough all by themselves, but we also had to rent all our ski equipment and everything. It seemed like all I had done so far was to watch the money run out of my pocket.

But finally we got ourselves in place on top of the mountain, ready to go. All we had to do was get into our skis.

Our kids were eight and ten at the time, neither one of them exactly able to handle this job on their own, so I was having to do everything for them. After working and working to get my son's gear on, I could already feel the temper and frustration rising up inside me. By the time I got to Stephanie, my daughter, my fuse was getting really short.

By forcing and pushing and shoving and squeezing, I finally got one of her feet into place. (Click.) But the other foot didn't go so well. We got it in there, all right, but when I tried securing the clamp, I couldn't get it to work correctly. It just sort of clunked. And the more we fiddled and fussed and fumed with it, the madder I got at her, at the heat, at this whole stupid idea for coming out here.

And while all of this was boiling inside me— suddenly, without warning—this ugly word slipped out.

I should stop and tell you that at the time, I was the cospeaker of Precept Ministries with Kay Arthur. I was cohost of a seven hundred-station radio program with Dr. Spiro Zodhiates, heard all over the nation. The church I was pastoring had been called one of the ten fastest growing congregations in the country. I was *somebody* in the spiritual world. (Ha!)

But for that frozen five seconds of time on a ski slope in the Rockies, I was the man who had just quieted the whole hillside with a four-letter profanity.

More than anything, however, I was the father whose ten-year-old daughter's mouth had just dropped open, stopping only long enough to gasp, "Dad!" on the way down.

Well, since we couldn't go any further because of her ski malfunction, we hopped the gondola and floated all the way back down to the lodge, where the instructor took one look at the problem, flicked one finger at the apparatus, and made me feel like one big fool for not knowing it was that easy to fix.

So back up the mountain we went, my daughter and I sitting facing each other, my eyes darting here and there, not wanting to make contact.

Then finally, with no other available way to avoid the discomfort, I sort of scratched my head and said, "Stephanie, honey, what you heard come out of my mouth up there is exactly who your daddy is apart from the saving grace of Jesus Christ."

We laughed. She knew.

But sometimes we Christians forget. We think we've gotten our flesh to a point where it's really not so bad after all. We've worked it and honed it and polished it up, made it presentable. We could come really close to telling you, in fact, that we think we've finally gotten beyond the problems that sin used to cause us.

What arrogance! Who do we think we are?

I know what Paul thought about himself. "What a wretched man I am!" he wrote for all the world to see. "Who will rescue me this body of death?" (Rom. 7:24).

That's a good question. And it's a good thing he asked it with a "who" at the beginning instead of a "what," because no "what" can get us out of this sin addiction we have—no formula, no plan, no pencil-and-notebook procedure, no massive revision of our daily schedule.

The only answer to this question is a "who," a person. And we all know "who" it is.

"I thank God through Jesus Christ our Lord" (v. 25).

Where Doubts Go to Die

I'm here to tell you from many years of experience: living the Christian life is not easy. This condition of ours—this daily struggle we continue to face with our sin nature and the law's demands—is one that can worry us into exhaustion.

How many times, in fact, has it made you doubt whether you're even saved?

• Let's say you can't seem to quit gossiping, cutting people down, being critical.

• You can't stop lusting, flipping to nasty TV shows when you're family's not looking.

• You can't stay out of the pantry, always choosing candy bars over carrot sticks.

• You can't make yourself forgive, even though the bitterness is tearing you up inside.

• You can't be consistent about reading your Bible. It just doesn't do it for you.

Every one of us struggles in our own sin areas, losing every bit as much or more often than we win. And it can make us wonder, "How could I be saved and still be so sinful?"

I assure you, that's not where Paul was going with this. The point of his discussion was not to make us feel like heathens. Nor was it to convince us that sin has more power over us than Christ does. That's a lie.

I know this because, before people came along and chopped the Bible up into chapters and verses (which I'm glad they did), Paul's next words after Romans 7 clearly followed the same train of thought he'd been steering toward all along. His sum response to our problem with sin and the law was that "no condemnation now exists for those in Christ Jesus, because the Spirit's law of life in Christ Jesus has set you free from the law of sin and of death" (Rom. 8:1–2).

The main point of the law, it seems, is to frustrate us. I'll admit, this seems like an odd, almost belligerent thing for God to do. But how else would we ever be ready to receive Christ's righteousness until we realized we had absolutely none in ourselves?

"What the law could not do since it was limited by the flesh, God did. He condemned sin in the flesh by sending His own Son in flesh like ours under sin's domain, and as a sin offering, in order that the law's requirement would be accomplished in us"—*in us!*—"who do not walk according to the flesh but according to the Spirit" (vv. 3–4).

This teaching of Paul's was not meant to fuss at and berate us, to make us feel worse than we already do. He wanted to help us take our eyes off our precious little selves and our petty little struggles and focus all of our attention on the one who has, can, and will perform His righteousness in us.

So we have two choices every day of our lives: law or grace.

• *If we choose the law*—performance, attainment, approval—we are also choosing condemnation, death, habitual frustration, and the absence of divine joy.

• *But if we choose grace*—submission, surrender, humility—we choose for ourselves the fruits of the Spirit, which cannot be *condemned* by Christ because they are *produced* by Christ.

So we can quit trying to do it ourselves now. In fact, as it says in Galatians 2:19, we can—and must—die "to the law" if we really want to be able to "live to God."

CHAPTER 4

Picture Yourself Here

[Having a Blast Enjoying God's Blessings]

I was down in Mississippi some time back with one of my good friends, George Hester, a guy who loves the outdoors as much as I do. He had invited me down there (as he often does), and I fully expected we'd be spending the time like always: hunting, fishing, and generally goofing around.

When I got there on this particular visit, I asked him, "George, what are we going to do today?"

"We're going to have some fun, Wayne. We're going to blow up beaver dams."

"Aw, you've got to be kidding me!" I said. "Why do you want to do that?"

It's not that George gets his jollies from watching small aquatic creatures learn how to fly. But when you raise trees for cash (like he does), and the beavers dam up the streams and creeks that run through your property, the flooding they cause can wipe out your crop over time. When all of that backwater settles into a wooded area and stays there long enough, it can kill whole trees. So in order to keep his stock healthy and thriving, George has taken to wading out into the water, trapping the beavers in their makeshift homes, and blowing their dams to smithereens!

Sounded like fun to me! So we hopped on his four-wheeler and roared down into the swamps.

I had never been this close to dynamite in my whole life, and I couldn't wait to see it in action! Everything he did with it fascinated me, especially watching him bury the charges underwater. (I had no idea you could do that.) I was ready for blastoff!

After he'd gotten everything in place like he wanted, he handed me about thirty feet of wires and told me to go stick them into the ground. This was to keep any static electricity from setting off the explosives prematurely. "And one more thing," he said. "Get behind a tree!"

"Aw, come on, George. I want to watch!"

"Wayne," he said, "we're going to be blowing things up into the air that are going to come flying right back down. Now get behind something so you won't get hurt."

I didn't like the idea, but I figured I'd better go along with it.

Once we were both set, he motioned for me to get ready, touched off the receptacles, and—after a few breathless seconds of delayed reaction—boom! Logs, leaves, and sand ruptured into the air. More importantly, the floodwaters that had been lying stagnant for weeks started flowing again, away from the tree trunks they had been polluting, back to the natural courses where they belonged.

We got to the next dam, and I said, "George, don't just put one stick in there. Let's do three!"

He did. This time, it wasn't just boom; it was B-O-O-O-O-O-M! Stuff shot a hundred feet into the air. And just like before, the water that had been puddled for weeks found its rightful path again, a way to do something productive with all of its potential and properties, not just to sit baking in its own slime.

Before we got finished that day, I had worked George up to five sticks of dynamite in one dam. It was incredible! And when he asked me back the next year—knowing I'd be expecting even more mayhem than before—he had concocted some kind of high-grade mixture in a big five-gallon can that he promised would "create a nuclear explosion." This big boy wasn't going after a beaver *dam* but a beaver *den!* The grandaddy of them all!

I know for a fact that the blast we ignited broke drinking glasses a quarter of a mile away, rattling them out of their cabinets and into the sink. I know, too, that nothing any bigger than the tip of my finger came out of that beaver hole!

But you know what else caught my eye . . . again? The water—slowly but surely regaining its movement, swirling out of its swamplike existence, coming out from under its pond scum and into a crystal flowing current.

I find that to be interesting, insightful into our spiritual lives.

Jesus said, "The one who believes in Me, as the Scripture has said, will have streams of living water flow from deep within him" (John 7:38).

You've heard this verse so many times, you might have been tempted to skim over it too fast. So go back. Read it again. And rest your eyes on the part that tells you where this "living water" flows.

It flows from "deep within" you. It's not something you have to go out and get. It's not something you've been lacking, a shortage that needs to be made up with extra infusions of God's grace and blessings. Oh, perhaps it's been dammed up by sin and compromise, by misguided assumptions about God and His love, by cycles of circumstances that have choked out your desire to keep believing.

But the water of God's Spirit is still there, just where it's always been. It's been there ever since you trusted Christ for salvation. It's been there, in fact, "from the foundation of the world" (Eph. 1:4), when your name was written "in the book of life" (Rev. 17:8).

Everything you need, Christ has already given you.

On the Inside Looking In

Many Christians today are trying to get into a room they're already in. Maybe one of those Christians is you.

Perhaps you believe that if you really had God's blessing on your life, you wouldn't feel as depressed and discouraged as you do.

Perhaps you know other believers who are just always up, who always seem to be in gear with God. It bothers you that you're not like them.

Perhaps you've been told that if you would just do this or that, if you'd embrace some particular teaching, if you'd enter through a different spiritual window or cut a new place in the wall, you could finally walk into the full experience of God's presence.

Oh, my friend, I know you're genuinely seeking God, simply wanting to live in the deepest, most vibrant relationship with Him that you can. I know you're wanting to honor Him and to let Him be glorified through your life. So please don't think I'm being trite or simplistic when I tell you this, but that room you're wanting to get into? That place of spiritual peace and possibility that all the super-Christians seem to be so at home in? That life of daily freedom and fellowship you'd give anything to find?

It's already yours.

You don't need a second blessing to unlock it. You already have the One who blesses—living inside you, right now!

You don't need to crack some kind of cosmic code or discover the three spiritual keys to lasting fulfillment. You already possess more power and provision than you can shake a stick at.

To ensure you I'm not making this up, let's spend a little time shaking some biblical trees to find out how much fruit will fall from their branches, to see how many blessings are already ours in Christ.

The Book of Ephesians is a good place to start counting.

According to God

We're going to be traveling through Paul's letter to the Ephesians for the next several chapters, so let's take a second to get our arms around it, to take in the big picture.

The hinge of Ephesians begins in verse 14 of chapter 3, where Paul says, "For this reason I bow my knees before the Father." This little section—this prayer that runs from verse 14 to verse 21—sums up chapters 1–3 and sets up chapters 4–6.

But what was this "reason" Paul talked about (v. 14) for bowing in reverence and praise to God? When you go hunting for the answer, you find yourself back at verse 1, where he began another sentence with the same words: "For this reason." Even at the beginning of chapter 3, he was still referring to something he'd said earlier.

Actually, I believe here in verse 1 of chapter 3, he was starting the prayer he never got around to until later in verse 14. But before he could get the words out of his mouth, he became so awed by the "mystery" of God's salvation to the Gentiles (v. 3), that he trailed off for another thirteen verses, imploring the Ephesian believers to stop and consider what an amazing gift they'd received.

So in order for us to locate Paul's "reason" for saying this, we still need to keep backtracking—back to verse 19 of Ephesians chapter 2, where Paul was summarizing everything he'd been saying from the very beginning of his letter.

"So then," he wrote to the Gentile church, "you are no longer foreigners and strangers, but fellow citizens with the saints, and members of God's household, built on the foundation of the apostles and prophets, with Christ Jesus Himself as the cornerstone. The whole building is being fitted together in Him and is growing into a holy sanctuary in the Lord, in whom you also are being built together for God's dwelling in the Spirit" (vv. 19–22).

Wow. What an amazing thing for a converted Jew to be celebrating! Knowing Paul's past as an archdefender of Jewish religious purity, only God could have given him the grace to enjoy the Gentiles' benefits in Christ.

Beyond that, Paul was writing to men and women who lived in a city that was running over with satanic, cult activities. The temple of Artemis, for example, was located in Ephesus. Pilgrims from far and wide converged on the city each spring to pay homage to this mother goddess of fertility.

Imagine what it meant to these early believers to be told—even in the midst of all this darkness, superstition, and false worship—that they were each "a holy temple" of the living God (2:21 NASB). When they walked around town, they carried the Spirit of the risen Christ inside them. And Paul was desperate for them to see what all this entailed, to help them grasp the truth of how much God had done for them.

From this passage, then, you can jump straight over to chapter 3 in Ephesians and better understand what he was trying to convince his readers of. "I pray that He may grant you, according to the riches of His glory, to be strengthened with power through His Spirit in the inner man . . . able to comprehend with all the saints what is the breadth and width, height and depth, and to know the Messiah's love that surpasses knowledge, so you may be filled with all the fullness of God" (vv. 16, 18–19).

Two phrases jump out here:

• *"I pray that He may grant you."* The word *grant* means to do something for another person in order to show your good intentions. Everything God does (or allows to happen) in our lives is an expression of His good and perfect will toward us. Paul not only wanted his readers to know what God had given them but why He had given it.

• *"According to the riches of His glory."* This little phrase—"according to"—plays a major role in the Book of Ephesians. In the New International Version, this phrase is wrongly interpreted as "out of." If that were correct, Paul would have used the Greek word *ek*. But the actual word used here wasn't *ek* but *kata*, which means "according to."

And there is a world of difference between the two.

Let's say, for example, that I had a million dollars. (I wish.) And I had determined to give you some money. Would you prefer for me to give you something *out of* my wealth or *according to* my wealth? If I give you a portion *out of* my wealth, I may just decide to give you a dollar. But if I give to you *according to* my wealth, my gift must reflect the full measure of what I possess.

It's easy to see, then, that we're a whole lot better off receiving "according to the riches of His glory" than getting just one little slice "out of" it. Thankfully, that's what the Bible actually says. And in order to understand Ephesians, it's absolutely key that you see this.

We're not talking about a God who deals in discounts and half measures. He doesn't do things on the cheap. Our God "is able to do above and beyond all that we ask or think—*according to* the power that works in you" (3:20)—"*according to* the working of His vast strength" (1:19).

See what I mean?

This is what takes your Christian life way beyond the routine and ordinary and zooms it right off the chart. You are being blessed and cared for "according to" God's infinite greatness.

The riches He has given you, therefore, are "unfathomable" (3:8 NASB), "unsearchable" (KJV), "incalculable."

After a million years in glory, you'll still be discovering new depths and facets to His blessings. They're like a well that has no bottom, an inexhaustible supply of resources, never turning up dry no matter how many times you dip your cup in for replenishment.

And because God has poured so much spiritual wealth into your life—just as He did for the Christians in Ephesus—Paul prayed "that the eyes of your heart may be enlightened so you may know what is the hope of His calling, what are the glorious riches of His inheritance among the saints" (1:18).

This bounty of blessing from God's hand is not something you can explain or figure out on your own. But when your spiritual senses have been "enlightened" by the Holy Spirit, when He pulls the chain that illuminates your mind and heart, revealing to you the full measure of God's grace and mercy freely lavished on you, you'll see at least a little bit of what He's given you. You'll marvel at the incredible lengths of His love.

You'll realize how blessed you already are.

Searching the Unsearchable: Ephesians 1

When something is described as "unsearchable" (the way God's riches are), that doesn't mean there's no sense in looking into them. Just because there's more food on the table than you could possibly eat doesn't mean you can't enjoy yourself and see how much you can hold.

Certainly, there's no end to the abundance of God He's invested in each of His children. But what a joy to be able to pick up a few of His blessings one by one and study them more closely, knowing full well that there are plenty more where these came from, waiting just beneath the surface, never to rust, retire, or run out.

So let's dive in feet first and see what we find.

Everything

"Blessed be the God and Father of our Lord Jesus Christ, who has blessed us with every spiritual blessing in the heavens, in Christ" (1:3).

Whoa, right off the bat, we've stumbled upon the First National Bank of all the blessings of God. But when do we receive this windfall of spiritual wealth? Is it something He'll give us down the road once we understand it all a little better? Is it something that won't really mature until we're finally in heaven with Him?

No, Paul said these are gifts of God He already "*has* blessed us with"—past tense, already happened, old news.

Take a minute to breathe this in! Many people have gotten their lives off center by not realizing this core, biblical truth. Christians by the thousands are still on the hunt for blessings they're pretty sure they haven't been able to access yet. They're not convinced they got it all when they received Christ.

Have you ever felt that way?

I'll tell you why I think this happens. It boils down to our confusion between *material* blessings and *spiritual* blessings.

When we possess a material blessing—and thank God He throws these in from time to time, when He sees fit to do so—we can see it with our own eyes. When we've gotten a new car, or a nicer house, or an extra amount in our savings account, it's not hard to quantify that.

Spiritual blessings, though, are a little different. Not only are they far greater than material blessings, but they also require a different set of sensors to detect their existence. These are not things that can be earned and attained; they can only be received. God produces them in our lives.

Let's look at it this way. True story. A woman called up a pastor friend of mine once and asked him to pray for her, telling him that she needed God to give her patience. (Who hasn't asked the Lord for that at least once in their lives?) My buddy answered her and said, "I don't think that's really what you want me to pray."

"Oh, yes, it is!" she replied. "I'm going through some terrible circumstances. Please, please, pray for me to have patience!"

"Why don't you let me pray for you another way?" he asked.

"No, no! Pray for me to have patience."

So, tired of trying to convince her otherwise, he began to pray as she asked him to: "Lord, just honoring Your Word, I pray that You'll intensify the pressure on this dear woman. I pray that she will soon be facing situations that are tougher than anything she's ever known in her entire life. I pray, Father, that whether it takes people or circumstances or whatever difficulty is required, You will allow enough challenges into her life to . . ."

"Whoa, whoa, whoa!" she screamed into the phone. "I asked you help me pray for patience."

"I am," he answered.

"What do you mean?"

"Romans 5:3," he said. "Tribulation worketh patience" (KJV).

I know this seems strange, but I assure you, that's the way spiritual blessings work. You don't sock them away in your back pocket, holding them in reserve for a rainy day. But when pressure comes from the outside, it forces out of you the power you have on the inside. When you need it, it's just there!

For example, you may not know you have patience in Christ until you come up against a matter that's pressing enough to require it. But when you go to Him, opening your heart to receive it and to let Him exercise it through you, there it is! You already have it!

It's not something that's sold in a self-help class. You don't have to go to a retreat center to get it. God simply produces it in your life, right when you need it, in ample supply to meet whatever situation you're facing.

Patience. Faith. Hope. Love. Humility. Kindness. Self-control. They're yours! You already have them! "Every spiritual blessing" is ours in Christ Jesus.

Now I'll tell you one thing I'm not particularly crazy about when it comes to this truth. It packs up every excuse you've ever thought of and throws it right out the window. Because when we have "every spiritual blessing in the heavens," there's not an excuse in the world we can lean on.

"I can't," for example, is automatically replaced by "He can."

But the bigger the crisis, the more certain the supply. The quicker we naturally turn to the "I can't" card, the more powerfully we get to experience what only "He can" do.

That's because in Him we have everything we need. Right now. Today. Already.

Everything.

Purpose

Another example of the unsearchable riches we've received in Christ is purpose, meaning, a reason for being here.

Paul expressed this truth in the very first verse of Ephesians, using a term that perhaps was clearer to his original readers than it is to those of us living with two thousand additional years of history behind us. In introducing his letter, he wrote, "Paul, an apostle of Christ Jesus by God's will: To the *saints* and believers in Christ Jesus" (1:1).

"Saint" comes from the word *hagios,* which carries the idea of being "set apart," put into a class all by ourselves, entrusted with an eternal purpose.

This doesn't mean we Christians are *better* than anybody else. Neither does it relieve us of the urgency for telling people about Christ. I mean, we want to encourage others to come be a part of this too! But it does mean that God's grace has set us apart for different uses than unbelievers—to draw attention and glory to Jesus Christ.

It's similar to what happens to us in marriage. Paul said that we husbands are to love our wives "just as Christ also loved the church and gave Himself up for her, so that He might *sanctify* her" (5:25–26 NASB). That word *sanctify* is from the same family as the word *saint,* meaning (again) "to set apart." The love Christ produces in me for my wife puts her in a class by herself. God's love reaches through me to meet the needs in her life, to make her relationship with me unique and special.

So a saint is *anyone* who is indwelled by the Spirit of God, *anyone* who has been transformed by the life of Christ. Every day when I crawl out of bed and look in the mirror, I have every right to answer back to that familiar, frumpy face of mine, "Good morning, saint!"

That's who I am in Christ.

I remember teaching this to a group of students in Indonesia, many of whom had traveled across the country to receive some additional training in biblical thought and principles. There were several hundred of them—the poorest, most deprived people I had ever been around. And when I encouraged them (through the translator) to see themselves as saints in Christ, they looked back at me with the emptiest expressions I had ever seen, like a calf staring at a new gate. Total incomprehension. Just . . . nothing.

As I came to find out, it wasn't merely my six-foot, seven-inch frame that caused them to feel smaller than they were, towering above their tiny Asian statures. My mere presence as an American represented to them—from years of ingrained attitudes and assumptions—that I had *everything* they wanted in life. I had more valuable possessions in my sock drawer than they had in their whole villages. I stood for money, possessions, and things—pleasures they coveted for their own. How could their meager lifestyles possibly qualify them as special in the eyes of the world, much less in the eyes of God?

But on the last day of our meeting, a breakthrough occurred. The Holy Spirit had spent the week "enlightening" them to their value in Christ Jesus. They had caught the reality that, although their feet may have been shod in sandals strapped together from loose string and tire treads, their lives were seated with Christ in heavenly places. They came to realize that God had visited them in their poverty and had poured out on them "every spiritual blessing" known to man. They were "saints" of God, not living beneath the standards of the rich and powerful but as full partners with all of God's people, infused with every bit as much meaning and purpose as anyone in the world.

Their faces that day said it all.

That's because it doesn't matter where you live, what you have, when you came to Christ, or how old you are. As long as there's breath in your body, God has a purpose for your life.

And this purpose of yours is found in daily surrender to Christ, letting Him be in you what you could never be on your own.

Our reason for being here is to reflect Christ to mankind, to bring recognition to Him as He lives His life in us. As the psalmist prayed, assured of the Lord's answer, "Even when I am old and gray, God, do not abandon me. Then I will proclaim Your power to another generation, Your strength to all who are to come" (Ps. 71:18).

Good morning, saint! It's a good day to be alive in Christ Jesus!

Acceptance

"He *chose* us in Him, before the foundation of the world, to be holy and blameless in His sight" (Eph. 1:4).

How do you like that?

"In love, He *predestined* us to be adopted through Jesus Christ for Himself, according to His favor and will" (vv. 4–5).

Oh, dear.

Now I'll tell you what: some people would love to see us get into a big argument over this, but I'm not one of them. I get to visit a lot of different churches every year as a conference speaker and so forth. I hear the long, drawn-out stories from the ones that are dividing into camps, not only splitting hairs but splitting their entire congregations apart over words and definitions.

Listen, I not only have no problem with the fact that I've been "chosen" and "predestined" by almighty God; I glory in the fact that He has condescended to reveal His grace to me.

I mean, there's no doubt that we receive our salvation through the deliberate, determined act of God. "You did not choose Me," Jesus said to His disciples, "but I chose you" (John 15:16). "There is no one who understands; there is no one who seeks God" on His own initiative (Rom. 3:11). You can't argue with that!

But doesn't the Bible also say, "Everyone who calls on the name of the Lord will be saved" (Rom. 10:13)? How much clearer can you get than "whosoever will, let him take the water of life freely" (Rev. 22:17 KJV)?

Look, it's a mystery. People can document their findings all they want in their position papers and such, but the Bible drops a plumb bob into the balance of this discussion. On one side is the election of God; on the other is the responsibility of man.

And I say, let them hang there.

Don't try to sway them.

If you move them one way or the other, you take them out of position and throw your theology off kilter.

So save yourself a lot of needless worry and headaches. Stop trying to figure out every detail, as though God's wisdom could compress itself into a small enough concept for our piddly little brains to figure out.

When someone asked Jesus, "Lord, are there few being saved?" (Luke 13:23), Jesus basically told Him to quit worrying about everybody else. "Make every effort," he said, "to enter through the narrow door" yourself (Luke 13:24). In other words, don't feel the need to borrow God's responsibility from Him, trying to carry it on your own shoulders. You've got more than enough to worry about with your own sinful flesh!

Let this matter of how salvation works just sit there. Let it hang. Let it be enough for you that before you ever breathed your first breath, before your heart ever beat one time, God knew you, loved you, and "chose" you.

I don't mean to make light of the doctrinal importance of God's effectual calling and His predestination. It's just that I don't see why all believers can't embrace this as a *good* thing. The Greek word for "predestination" is *proorizo,* which basically means "to make a decision beforehand based on knowledge you already have." Who better to make these eternal decisions than the One who possesses all knowledge in Himself and sees all things perfectly?

As my friend Dr. Spiro Zodhiates says, I consider this to be a "secret of the family." Even the *Westminster Confession of Faith,* the compendium of Calvinist theology, states, "The doctrine of this high mystery of predestination is to be handled with special prudence and care." We don't quite understand it, but we treasure it as an indispensable part of our heritage and destiny. "How unsearchable His judgments and untraceable His ways!" (Rom. 11:33).

"The hidden things belong to the LORD our God, but the revealed things belong to us and our children forever" (Deut. 29:29). And among those things we *do* understand is that God's choosing us means He has not rejected us, though we are more than worthy of His wrath.

Each of us—every single one of us—has been born into the most dysfunctional family of all: the accursed bloodline of Adam. Yet although nothing in us is capable of producing pleasure or approval in the eyes of God, He has chosen in Christ to adopt us as His sons and daughters.

"For those He foreknew He also predestined to be conformed to the image of His Son, so that He would be the first among many brothers" (Rom. 8:29). Therefore, we are as safe and protected in this family of God as the Son himself is at the right hand of the Father.

For "those He predestined, He also called; and those He called, He also justified." *But wait! He's not finished with us yet!* "Those He justified, He also glorified" (Rom. 8:30). The process of our salvation—though already complete in Christ—is still going on. It awaits our glorification, the resurrection of our bodies into a heavenly state.

What makes us think, then, that he would dispose of us along the way? Why would he ever lop us off in midstream after already investing so much of Himself in us?

In the Greek world inhabited by the Ephesians, a father who adopted a son into his family was forbidden by law from rejecting him and casting him out of his home. Is it possible, then, that what a pagan father *couldn't* do, our heavenly Father *would?*

You are precious to God. He chose you for His own.

Redemption

Not only are we the recipients of "every spiritual blessing," saints chosen by God "to the praise of the glory of His grace, which He freely bestowed on us in the Beloved" (Eph. 1:6 NASB), we are also *redeemed* through Christ's blood and *forgiven* of our sins (v. 7).

Redemption comes from two words in the Greek: *apo,* meaning "away from," and *lutrosis,* meaning "to purchase." Those in the ancient world would have quickly understood the word picture. It speaks of what happened when some helpless man or woman, boy or girl, was purchased off the slave block, released from the power of those who held them bound and without freedom.

Most of us limit redemption in our minds to the mere act of salvation, the transaction that occurred releasing us from the sin debt we owed. But oh, it is much more than that!

God's redemption not only freed us from the *penalty* but also the *power* of sin. Through His grace we have not only been saved from our past mistakes but secured against any and all future slipups. The only reason we sin against God as believers is because we choose to do so, not because we are any longer under sin's controlling thumb. His redemption covers our lives in all directions.

Let me tell you how I know this: Paul went on to say that God had given us these blessings—redemption and forgiveness—*"according to* the riches of His grace" (v. 7). Remember that little phrase "according to"? This assures us that no legal loopholes or second opinions can ever intervene to disrupt the flow of God's grace into our lives. We are both liberated and empowered by the inexhaustible flow of His living grace.

Protection

Another of the blessings Paul mentioned, which we mustn't let slip into insignificance merely because of our differences in culture and understanding, is the fact that we have been "sealed with the promised Holy Spirit" (v. 13).

The word for "sealed" is *sphragizo,* which means "to put a mark on someone or something, causing it to be authentic." It's kind of like a brand, a mark of ownership.

You see it all over the place in Scripture. As far back as the Book of Genesis, a seal or signet ring was used to identify property or documents. Throughout the annals of Israelite history, seals were often employed to authenticate letters, bind covenants, and engrave inscriptions. People in Bible days knew full well what a seal was and meant.

And still today you and I and all those who have trusted in Christ for salvation bear the signifying mark of the Holy Spirit. We are known by the difference His presence makes in our lives. He is the undeniable proof that our hearts have been captured by the amazing grace of God.

Anyone masquerading as a believer without coming through the cross of Christ is missing the one thing that authenticates him and declares him to be genuine. "But if the Spirit of Him who raised Jesus from the dead dwells in you, He who raised Christ from the dead will also give life to your mortal bodies through His Spirit who dwells in you" (Rom. 8:11).

That's a promise—a covenant that doesn't just work for us up until today or the next time we do something to tick God off really bad. We are sealed, Paul said, "for the day of redemption" (Eph. 4:30). If we are filled and marked and branded by God's Spirit today, then we are assured of being "sealed" and protected from now until eternity.

All Power

As if blessings like these weren't enough—as if we should be concerned that God's "everything" promise runs the risk of disappointing us (like everything else in life tends to do)—Paul reminds us that the Christ who delivers all these blessings to us dwells "far above every ruler and authority" (Eph. 1:21).

That's saying a lot.

More than that, however, he's also "far above every . . . power and dominion."

Bigger than presidents, dictators, and even long-bearded terrorists.

And if you need any more convincing, if this world still seems like a daunting place for God to carry out His promises, be assured that He's "far above . . . every title given, not only in this age but also in the one to come."

Are you listening to this, devil?

Did you know that Jesus, every second that He lived on the earth, had the power to call "legions" of angels to His side in order to shut up His critics and even stop the crucifixion? Countless heavenly messengers were waiting on tiptoe, ready to lunge at the sound of His voice.

That's power, my friend. And the ability to restrain Himself from using it? That's power raised to the *ultimate* power!

But you know what else? When the time is finally right, when God in His wisdom decides to give the command for Satan's little playtime on earth to come to an end, how many angels is He going to dispatch for this colossal assignment?

Uh, one. (That answer will save you a trip to Revelation 20.)

Not Michael. Not Gabriel. Not one of the big-name beings. Just an ordinary, run-of-the-mill, standard-issue angel. But you can be sure he'll have more than enough strength to tie Satan hand and foot, chain him up in the pits of hell, and make sure the lock is tight enough for him never to get out.

There's no defining the kind of power God has. "Immeasurable greatness" is as close as Paul could come to putting a stopwatch or a yardstick on it (v. 19). God "demonstrated this power in the Messiah by raising Him from the dead and seating Him at His right hand in the heavens" (v. 20).

And now this surpassing power flows through us . . . as we submit and surrender to His work in our lives. Our strength never comes from muscling out a lot of sweat and effort for God. Our wisdom never arrives from drawing up our own plans on a chalkboard in a committee meeting. The Spirit and the blessings of God flow through us only as we remain "seated . . . with Him in the heavens" (Eph. 2:6).

Yes, seated . . . remembering who's boss, remembering who's God, remembering where our strength comes from.

Stephen, the first Christian martyr, experienced this.

Was Stephen able in his own power to stand before the jeering mob intent on burying him under a mountain of rocks? Did he know without a doubt that he had the courage within himself to articulate a rational defense of his faith under the threat of immediate death? Was he sure going in that he had enough love in his heart to forgive those who thought they were doing God's work by spilling his blood?

If he had taken matters into his own hands, who knows? His story might not have factored so prominently into the faith-filled history of the early church. But because he was willing to keep his life submitted, his will suppressed, his heart seated in surrender to Christ, he got to see an amazing thing.

For when the tempers had flared to their highest pitch, when the pain of the blows had reached unbearable proportions, when the nightmare of his own violent death had become an inescapable reality, God peeled back the curtain for him between heaven and earth. And Stephen saw a strange sight.

His Lord was no longer seated at the right hand of the Father. "Look!" he exclaimed. "I see the heavens opened and the Son of Man *standing* at the right hand of God!" (Acts 7:56).

Oh, man . . . that's power!

When times come around in your life that outmatch your ability to endure them, stay seated in your rightful place, with Him as your head, your Lord, your Master. Yes, keep your seat, assured that you already have "every spiritual blessing" in Christ.

And let Jesus do the standing.

That's when the "living water" really starts to flow.

CHAPTER 5

Down Home with Jesus

[Appropriating What You Already Have in Christ]

I'm thankful for chapter breaks. I really am. If this book had been nothing other than one long, unbroken essay, I'm sure you'd have never made it this far.

Neither would I.

But I just want to remind you that these three chapters—4, 5, and 6—are all based on the Book of Ephesians. And they all interrelate. So before we get too deep into this one, be sure to remember what we talked about in the last one. You have "every spiritual blessing" in Christ, and don't you ever forget it!

It's one thing, however, to *know* this truth; it's another to *live* it. We can be mentally convinced and aware that we possess all things in Christ, but that's not the same as walking in His fullness.

I'll give you a little example of this. I had made plans one afternoon to go hit a few buckets of golf balls at a nearby driving range. I was going to be playing in a tournament later in the week, and some friends and I had arranged a time and place to get together, just to practice and have some fun.

Now don't take from this that I'm some kind of crackerjack golfer. I'm not! I can play just enough to get by and that's about it. Of course, if golf was like most *normal* sports, where the guy who scores the most points wins, I'd be a real force to be reckoned with. But . . .

One thing I'd forgotten that day was that I was going to be dropping off my car at the repair shop. So the car I'd be driving in the afternoon when I came home to change clothes was going to be one I had borrowed from someone else. My car, my keys, and my garage door opener would all be up on a grease rack across town.

The reality of this hit me just as I was pulling into the driveway at about a quarter till four. I knew that my wife, Diana, wasn't at home and wouldn't be for some time. *But surely,* I thought, masterminding a plan while standing flat-footed at the front door, *surely there's some way I can get in here!*

Let me say that from that day to this, I have not lost one minute's sleep worrying about whether someone might break into my house. I mean, even with prior, inside knowledge on where every possible point of entry was, I couldn't break into my own home!

So there I stood, cupping my hands against the little windows on my garage door, peering in at everything I needed in order to meet my friends at the driving range. My golf bag was there with all my clubs inside it. My golf shoes were there, all ready to go.

They were mine! I could prove it! And I was less than ten feet away from them!

But what difference did it make, as long as something was standing in the way between me and my possessions?

You could think of a dozen other ways to describe this. It's like driving up to an ATM, trying to withdraw money out of your own banking account, yet not being able to remember your PIN number.

It's like standing at a soft drink machine holding a twenty-dollar bill. You've got way more than enough to pay for the can of Coke you want, but you can't put paper money in a coin slot.

It's like being on your cell phone, sitting in your car, needing to jot a note to yourself, yet not being able to find anything to write with except a pencil that's never been sharpened. You've got plenty of lead there— enough to write *ten thousand* times what you need, but there's no point in even trying.

This is the kind of frustration felt by far too many Christians—believers who feel pretty sure that God has blessed them with everything they'll ever need in Him but who don't know how to appropriate what they've been given.

Good thing for us, though, Paul was all over this in his letter to the Ephesians.

As I said in the last chapter, Paul's prayer at the end of Ephesians 3 is the focal point of the whole book. It's the key to helping us understand how to unlock the unsearchable riches of God's grace.

Inner Workings

The best way I know to explain my point is just to let the Bible speak, verse by verse, word by word. People can argue with me about this all they want—and they do—but each of us ultimately must come to terms with the Word of God. Right?

People tell me, for example, that the grace-filled life is too passive, that it gives us permission to underachieve and not even care about it.

They tell me it preaches a smug, overly self-confident form of superiority, that it makes people feel as if they've arrived and have no more room for growth.

They tell me it sets people up for disappointment, that it makes them think their struggles will all be over once they embrace this lifestyle and mind-set.

None of this is true.

The Christian life is incredibly difficult. None of us ever gets a total handle on it. And our battle against sin and the flesh will rage on until the day we die.

But with all of that said, the Bible is clear that God has given us an honest-to-goodness way to walk in genuine victory, to experience and enjoy the blessings that flow from His hand. He has painted for us in His Word a picture of the normal Christian life—the way we're supposed to live it.

It begins by realizing (as we discussed in the last chapter) that God has already given us everything we need by virtue of our relationship with Jesus Christ. Peter said it this way: "His divine power has given us *everything* required for life and godliness, through the knowledge of Him who called us by His own glory and goodness" (2 Pet. 1:3).

What else can *everything* mean but "everything"? God has given His people "everything required" for both "life" (our inward relationship with Christ) and "godliness" (our outward expression of obedience and gratitude).

Again, I'm not saying for one minute that this completeness comes from our own strength or imagination. Although Christ has indeed given us everything, we can do nothing without Him (John 15:5). It's all about Jesus, not about us.

This was precisely the point Paul was making in Ephesians 3. And verse 16 is a good place to start seeing it: "I pray that He may grant you, according to the riches of His glory, to be strengthened with power *through His Spirit* in the inner man."

Key in also on some other important words:

"Strengthened." This not only carries the obvious meaning but also has the idea of being "put on display" as being strong, not just when someone hears all our spiritual sounding *talk* but when they actually notice the way we *live.* They recognize we have something not everyone else has—a strength, a depth, a noticeable inner resource.

"Power." This is the Greek word *dunamis,* from which we get our English words *dynamite* and *dynamo.* Dynamite, of course, is an explosive, immediate kind of power. It shows up in flashes of unleashed energy, targeted to meet a specific purpose. A dynamo, on the other hand, is a consistent source of ongoing power. *Staying power,* some might call it. Both of these expressions have their place in the Christian life, and both are

initiated, not by us, but by the Spirit who dwells in our . . .

"Inner man." All of this is happening "through" or "by means of" the Spirit of God, not through our own efforts or initiative. Furthermore, all this spiritual strengthening and empowering is happening on the inside, not out here on the surface where we judge everything based on physical strength and appearance.

In contrast to this "inner man" of ours, the "outer man" (in case you hadn't noticed) is "decaying" (2 Cor. 4:16 NASB). The hair is turning gray, where it's not turning loose. The muscles and joints are becoming stiff and unresponsive. The toenails are getting long and ugly. We do our best to keep it all under control, under wraps, under twenty dollars a week in various goos and ointments and lotions and stuff. But it's not always a pretty sight. And people who dare to be honest with themselves about it can see it happening with their own two eyes.

I remember several years ago my wife bought one of those mirrors that magnify your face about thirty-two times. (I'll never understand why anyone really wants to see that!) I came out of the shower one day, discovered this new mirror sitting there in the bathroom, and located enough splotches and blemishes on my face to start their own colony.

That kind of revelation is simply not interesting to me. I could go on just fine without ever knowing what my skin and body look like under that level of scrutiny.

Yet it should come as no big surprise to us that we're slowly wearing out, running down, washing up. The reason this is bearable, however—especially for believers in Christ—is because "though our outer man is decaying, yet our inner man is being renewed day by day" (2 Cor. 4:16 NASB).

This gets us back to the whole idea of religion versus Christianity:

- Religion is what we do *externally* to please God.
- Christianity is what He does *internally* through us.

If we were built for religion, then why in the world would God go to the trouble of placing His omnipotent Holy Spirit within us? What would be the point? Would the Spirit just be there for reinforcement? Would He be on standby for those moments when we get ourselves into a real jam?

The Christian life is not just *hard* without Christ; it's *impossible!* We can't do *anything* on our own that pleases God. But with Him inside us, enlivening us, working through us, we have dynamite power in the palm of our hands.

What's the Devil?

I want to stop here long enough to say that this truth—the fact that God has strengthened us with *His* power, according to the riches of *His* glory—should be enough to convince us that no power on earth can defeat us in Christ.

Oh, I don't have any illusions about my own strength. Even a sissy demon could make short work of me. But what can he do to the one who's seated above all power, names, and rule? If a demon were to try tangling with me, it wouldn't really be *me* he was up against. It would be the King of kings and the Lord of lords, the destroyer of demons.

A lot of churches out there are spending a lot of time trying to sniff out the devil's strongholds, binding and loosing and scrapping and clawing. This is distressing to me because in Ephesians 6, where Paul went to great lengths to teach us about spiritual warfare, he never once told us to go out there and pursue the devil. All he said was to "be strong in the Lord and in the strength of His might" (v. 10 NASB). We're not told to chase the devil down but to "stand firm against" his tactics and schemes (v. 11 NASB), dressed in the armor of God, which is Christ in us.

I just believe, whether it's unwillingness or false humility or fear or whatever it is that keeps us from realizing the riches we possess in Christ, these feelings produce the opposite effect of making Satan seem bigger in our eyes than he actually is. *He is a defeated foe!* If he ever catches up to you, what's he going to be able to do with you? Gum you to death?

I was in a meeting once where the host pastor came out every single night saying the same thing, always in a hushed, haunting voice: "Do you . . . sense him?"

I looked at the guy who was with me and said, "Is he talking about *you* or *me?*"

The pastor went on: "The devil's here. We need to bind him."

I thought to myself, *We just bound him last night. How'd that sucker get loose already?*

This happened in one form or another every night. All week long this pastor started every meeting by focusing on the devil. At the beginning of one service, he even wanted to open up a window to give the demons an easier exit from the sanctuary.

Part of me, I admit, was just sort of irritated by it. Yet I found myself asking the Lord to help me know how to approach this man, hoping for an opportunity to set him straight with some biblical counsel. I certainly didn't want to offend him. Neither did I want to come across as being haughty or superior in any way. I knew then—and still know today—that I had no authority on my own to make any claims about what was right or wrong. My only desire was to let the Word of God come to bear on this situation.

Interestingly enough, while several of us were eating dinner together one evening, this pastor turned to me, looked me straight in the eye, and said, "Preacher, can you tell me anything that would help me be a better pastor of this church?"

Have you ever had God open a door that wide for you? I mean, *anybody* could've spotted this one. I could have driven a Mack truck through it sideways!

So I said, "Let me just share this: I don't know all there is to know . . . by a long shot. But if I were you, I would never start another worship service again by making even one mention of the devil. He loves recognition any way he can get it. Our job as pastors is just to lift up Christ."

What happened then, I wasn't expecting. The next voice I heard was that of his wife, who sort of clanked her fork to the plate, sat back, smacked both hands to the table, turned to her husband, and said, "Well, thank God, somebody finally told you."

Uh-oh.

"What do you mean, honey?" he blurted out.

She said, "You've got these people scared half to death! There are little widows in this church who are afraid to go home at night. They call the deacons to come over and walk around their houses, pleading the blood of Jesus over every window and door frame before they can feel safe enough to go to sleep."

It was pretty intense, let me tell you. And although I know not everyone is quite as hung up on casting things out as this guy was, our overemphasis on all things demonic is a major source of fear and defeat today in the body of Christ.

Paul said in Ephesians 5:8: "You were once darkness, but now you are light in the Lord. Walk as children of light." Can darkness keep light from invading its space? No way. Instead, wherever light appears, the darkness has no choice but to back off and fade away. If the one whose Spirit lives in you—He who is the head of the body, the ruler of all—has shed His own light abroad in your heart, what can darkness do to you?

Understand who lives in you! Understand that you are already victorious in Him. You don't have to go around begging Him for victory. *You already have it!* And the key to appropriating it—the key to living in Christ's strength and power—is the same key you used when you received it.

Surrender. Submission. Trust. Grace. Faith.

Down Home

"[I pray] . . . that the Messiah may dwell in your hearts through faith" (Eph. 3:16–17).

The word for "dwell" in verse 17 does not have the same meaning as "*in*dwell," which is what Christ did for us at salvation. Instead, it's the word *kataoikeo*, which comes from two words: *kata,* meaning "down," and *oikeo,* meaning "house" or "home."

This is so important. Don't miss this!

We appropriate the strength and power of Christ in our lives as we accommodate Him in our hearts by faith, as we honor Him by obeying His Word, we make Him feel "down home."

Have you ever been in someone's house but not felt at home? Maybe it was decorated too ornately, filled with things you were afraid you'd break if you made one wrong move. Maybe the chairs and furniture were hard and uncomfortable. Maybe the people who lived there acted like you were keeping them up, bothering them. It was obvious that they'd really prefer it if you weren't around.

But I'm sure you've also walked into people's houses where they made you feel instantly welcomed, not just *at* home but *down* home. Totally relaxed and at ease. Maybe they pulled out a big slice of cake and set it right in front of you, the kind they knew you were partial to. Maybe they'd thought ahead and put some of your favorite magazines in the room where you'd be staying. You could tell from the looks on their faces that you were making their day just by being there.

Folks, this is what it's all about—accommodating the divine presence of God in our lives, giving Him any room He wants, any time He wants it. Making Him feel totally comfortable living inside us.

That's when we become "strengthened with power" —once we've backed away from showing off our own houses and dressing up our own façades, once we've discovered the only thing that makes our place special is the fact that Jesus has chosen to live there.

Home Is Where Your Heart Is

This happens, Paul said, in our "hearts." It's in our hearts that we're able to make Christ feel either down home or downplayed.

Perhaps, then, we need to look around our hearts for a minute, and see what kind of rooms are in there for God to "dwell in."

One of them is our *thoughts*. Luke told of a time when the disciples were arguing among themselves—beyond earshot from where Jesus could hear—about which of them would ultimately be the greatest in the kingdom of God. But Jesus, even without hearing them, knew "the thoughts of their *hearts*" (Luke 9:47).

You might ask, "Shouldn't Luke have said Jesus knew the thoughts of their *minds*?" Not according to the well-known twelfth verse of Hebrews 4: "For the word of God is living and active and sharper than any two-edged sword, and piercing as far as the division of soul and spirit, of both joints and marrow, and able to judge *the thoughts and intentions of the heart*" (NASB).

This verse gives parallel weight to three different aspects of the human makeup:

What gives life to the soul? The spirit.

What gives life to the bones? The marrow.

What gives life to our thoughts? Our hearts.

So when we're having trouble controlling the things we think about and dwell on, allowing them to wander into areas that are fearful, doubtful, lustful, or whatever, we don't really have a *mind* problem. We have a *heart* problem. We haven't chosen to create an environment in our thoughts where Jesus can live and work.

Another room is our *attitudes.* Remember Jesus' parable about the slave who was forgiven an enormous debt, only to go out and demand payment from someone else on a much smaller IOU? Jesus, in defending the master's judgment against the ungrateful servant, said, "My heavenly Father will also do the same to you, if each of you does not forgive his brother from *your heart*" (Matt. 18:35 NASB).

Again, the word "heart" seems almost out of place here. We think we forgive people with our mouths, right? They tell us they're sorry; we tell them not to mention it. We forgive them with our words.

How many of us, though, have stood between two children, ordering one to apologize to the other, only to hear the words "I'm sorry" and "That's OK" forced out through such strongly gritted teeth, we almost wished they hadn't said anything at all?

We grown-ups aren't really all that different sometimes. We may mask it a little better for public consumption, but we know the difference between forgiving someone with our words and truly forgiving them with our hearts. Our attitudes can only be Christ's when they come from a place deeper than mere syllables and stiff upper lips.

A third room in the heart is our *emotions.* Jesus said, "Your *heart* must not be troubled. Believe in God; believe also in Me" (John 14:1). The word for "troubled" is the word *tarasso,* which means "to be disturbed, frightened, or stirred up."

Today we'd call that stress. And by now every one of us has been around it long enough to know that we don't eliminate stress by fighting it, shoving it down, or just wishing it would go away. There are simply too many things that contribute to its presence. We can shut it off in one area, but life will find a way to worm it in from somewhere else.

According to the words of Jesus, though, belief in him is our only remedy for dealing with the stress in our lives. A heart that truly believes, that sees beyond the present and into eternity, that trusts in the love and sovereignty of almighty God, gives Him room to do what we could never do ourselves. When He is at home in our emotions, we can feel it even in our bones and our blood pressure. His welcome presence in our hearts soothes and heals us from the inside out.

You Want It When?

Your thoughts. Your attitudes. Your emotions. Of these three rooms that Christ wants to occupy in your heart, how many of them are you having a hard time making Him feel welcome in? Inside each one, in fact, how many nooks and crannies exist that you'd just as soon Jesus wouldn't look at? How hard would you bristle if Jesus asked to see under the bed, in the attic, or behind the closet doors of your heart?

And so, the question is, where do we even begin to start cleaning this place up?

I want to give you some good news. Start by thinking back to a time when your house had gotten into such chaos and disarray you didn't know how you'd ever get it under control again. Company was coming for the weekend perhaps, and you needed to act fast. What did you do? Clean up every room all at once?

When Christ convicts you of the need to welcome His presence into your whole heart, the thought of making that many changes at one time is daunting, to say the least. The legalist in us—the part of us that wants to do everything perfectly in our own strength—has every intention of growing ten sets of arms and legs to knock out the problem by this afternoon so we can brag about our accomplishments at prayer meeting tonight.

But those of us who are learning to live and breathe and feed on Christ's living grace are able to surrender our desire to fix this ourselves. Sure, our list of problem areas could easily run the length of this page. But to begin succeeding in this, we must start by simply accommodating Christ in the one or two places where we're having the hardest time wanting Him around right now.

I don't have to tell you what those key areas are in your life. You know what they are without thinking. Maybe it's sexual temptation. Maybe it's worry. Maybe it's doubts about God's love and compassion toward you. Again, you know exactly what your own sticky spot is at the moment.

Start there and . . .

• Tell God in prayer that you realize just how weak and powerless your flesh is, especially (it seems) in this particular aspect of your life.

• Thank Him for already filling you full of Himself, giving you everything you'll ever need in order to experience victory in your Christian walk.

• Submit to everything you know the Scripture teaches about what godliness looks like in this area, aligning your expectations with the Word of God.

• And then, just make Christ welcome there. Ask Him for the grace to *want* Him inside, to give Him the keys to your thoughts, attitudes, and emotions.

Again, this is not easy. You won't do it perfectly every time. But He will show you day by day through experience that, as you surrender to Him, He will strengthen you "with power . . . in the inner man." I guarantee it.

It's the same way He worked through the children of Israel in the early days of their history. God assured them He had already given them the land of promise— all of it—but they didn't just move in overnight. If they had, they couldn't have stood it! Instead, they came into the experience one day at a time—a setback here, a victory there. Yet when they looked back after full lifetimes of entering in, they discovered it was theirs! God had given them everything!

I assure you, the life of grace is not about arrival; it's about pursuit. It's not a method or formula we understand in our heads through study; it's an active strengthening we experience in our hearts through submission.

It starts and it grows. And the more we realize how Christ is overwhelming us with His own thoughts, attitudes, and emotions, the more we want of Him. Oh, the law would love to come back in, making us want to dig these behaviors out on our own, demanding that we get extra credit for our stellar accomplishments.

But that's when we must submit all the more, moment by moment, making sure our hearts are the kind of homes where we'd be happy for Jesus to sit next to us on the sofa. We need to prepare a place for *Him* until the day we enter into the place He's prepared for *us* (John 14:2).

Why Do We Do What We Do?

What motivates us, though, to move in this direction? What makes us want to get out of bed in the morning, ready to hop to it, itching to let Christ have every room in the house?

Throughout much of our lives, perhaps, we were motivated by *fear*. We served God out of dread for what might happen if we didn't. We saw Him as a snarling God who'd just as soon rap us across the head as look at us. We spent our lives constantly looking behind us, afraid we weren't doing everything good enough, fast enough, willingly enough.

Maybe, however, we've been driven by *guilt*. Trying hard to make amends for the pain we've caused Christ, our family, and others, we've pushed ourselves hard to pay for our sins, to make up for lost time, to prove to God that we *mean* it this go-around. I've even met missionaries on the foreign field who confessed to me that their decisions to enter high-risk Christian vocation was primarily based on guilt over their past.

Fear and guilt are the stock-in-trade of the law. They get results, at times, but at the high cost of spiritual exhaustion and sagging hearts.

Listen, then, to the words of Paul, expressing to us the heart of the Father:

"I pray that you, being rooted and firmly established *in love,* may be able to comprehend with all the saints what is the breadth and width, height and depth, and to know the Messiah's love that surpasses knowledge, so you may be filled with all the fullness of God" (Eph. 3:17–19).

His love is what motivates us. This is crystal clear. Look at the words Paul employed to encourage us in this:

Root yourself in it. Let His love be for you what nourishes and supplies your soul. Be constantly drawing life from His Word and His truth—the truth that God loved you in Christ before the beginning of time.

Ground yourself in it. Roots not only give health to a tree; they also provide its support and strength, protecting it from being easily toppled in a windstorm. Christ's love is what anchors and sustains us.

Measure its boundaries. Trust in the fact that His love for you truly has no limit, no end, no potential shortage of supply. You don't have to work to earn His love; he has already given it to you in fullness.

It is God's long-standing love that enables us freely to submit to Him, knowing deep within our hearts that we are placing ourselves in good hands—the best, the only hands that can lead us to lives of spiritual plenty and purpose.

So we should never think that we can pull out of context (as we often do) the great promise of verses 20–21 in Ephesians chapter 3: "Now to Him who is able to do above and beyond all that we ask or think—according to the power that works in you—to Him be glory in the church and in Christ Jesus to all generations, forever and ever."

Yes, He is certainly "able to do above and beyond all that we ask or think." But He does it only through lives that are submitted to Him, secure in Him, and satisfied in Him.

Who knows what all He could do in our hearts if we were to go out of our way each day to make a home for Him there?

Practically Speaking

I hope you're seeing how the message of grace quickly moves from doctrine and theology to practical living. We never want to separate it, of course, from its biblical foundations, but we must never be deceived into thinking God's truth is somehow unhinged from Monday morning experience.

This is precisely the pattern Paul used in the Book of Ephesians.

Throughout chapters 1–3, he was building the base, laying the groundwork, teaching us the eternal realities that form the foundation of Christian living. But beginning in chapter 4, he started showing us what can happen in our lives as a result, as we continue to surrender ourselves to Christ through faith.

Listen to Paul speaking, changing gears, and drawing conclusions: "I, therefore, the prisoner of the Lord, urge you to walk worthy of the calling you have received" (Eph. 4:1).

Poor old Paul. Still a prisoner after all these years. Yet what better picture of the grace of God could he have given us? Think of how enriched our lives have become as a result of what Christ did in Paul's heart during those long stretches in jail. During this same time of imprisonment, in fact, Paul wrote not only Ephesians but also the Books of Philippians, Colossians, and Philemon.

What if Paul had wasted all those lonely hours moping around, feeling sorry for himself, bent on revenge? What if he had decided in his heart that Christ could go live somewhere else, if that's the best he could do for people who were trying to work for Him?

But in full surrender—perhaps a deeper level of submission than he could have ever experienced had he been left free to wander and work and do as he pleased—God taught Paul what it meant to take himself out of the way so that Christ could have first place, the only place.

Paul's admonishment to us in the first verse of chapter 4 is for us to walk "worthy" of our calling. This is the Greek word *axios,* which describes a set of scales in perfect balance. Paul was reminding us that our workaday lives must equal out with the truths we hear on Sunday morning. These two aspects—knowledge and practice—should line up in the same direction and proportion.

In other words, our walk should match our talk.

But don't hear these familiar "walk the talk" words with the same ears you've heard them with before. Don't make the mistake of receiving this as a call to duty, a summons to buck up and start living right. Listen, this is not a marching order. *It's an invitation to submit your heart to Christ,* to exercise afresh the complete faith and trust you placed in Him the day you were saved.

I can't tell you how essential this is in taking the pressure off your life. If you regularly surrender your heart to Christ, you won't have to worry about drawing up a plan to ensure that your walk and your talk join forces together. Godly living will simply be the natural effect the grace-filled life has on you.

You'll start seeing things happening in your heart like those mentioned in verse 2:

Humility. This is the combination of two words that basically mean the mind-set of getting as flat on the ground as you can, knowing there is nothing about you that is worthy. This is one of those fruits of the Spirit that Jesus begins growing in you as you see yourself in the light of who he is.

Actually, you probably won't ever wake up and say, "Boy howdy, I sure am getting more humble." I suppose recognizing your own humility is probably the *opposite* of humility. But you *will* sense over time that the things you once took such pride in for yourself are now genuinely deflected to Christ . . . not through words designed to sound spiritual but from a heart that truly wants Him to get all the glory.

Gentleness. This doesn't mean sweetness as much as it means brokenness. It's like a horse that's been broken, with all of its power now harnessed and put under the control of its rider. Sure, the horse could kick up and flex its speed in any direction it wanted to go, but it's been trained over time to let the master work the reins.

We, too, have the full capability of choosing our own course and heading off that way ourselves. But what joy and purpose we discover when we allow Christ to ·lead, when in trust and surrender, our ways become His ways, whatever He wants. Our rights become His desires, wherever He chooses to take us.

Patience. The original word for this, *makrothumia,* means "long-suffering." And that's about as good a definition as we could ever want for patience. It's the supernatural ability to put up with those who are not lovable. And oh, how many times in an average week do we need this attribute in action in our lives!

We've all learned through hard experience that the Christlike characteristic of patience is not inherently resident in our human hearts. But how precious it is to feel it welling up inside us as Christ not only holds back our sharp words and snide remarks but also gives us genuine, long-suffering love for the hard to like.

Forbearance. This word, coming from the Greek *anecho,* means "to hold up or bear with." You could say it means "to hold each other up." Again we don't have to possess a great memory to recall times when we quit on other people, when instead of giving them time to calm down and come around, we cast immediate judgment and crossed them off our list of friends.

But when the forbearance of Christ is given room to work in our surrendered hearts, he changes us into people who no longer just fight and walk away. Instead, we stick with those who are rebelling against both the Lord and sound logic, the same way Christ has stuck with us over the years.

These are all *relationship words*—humility, gentleness, patience, forbearance. They are terms that define what's different about those who let Christ express Himself through them and toward others. When our hearts are surrendered, when we are continually living and leaning on His grace, our interactions with others and our response to difficulty is transformed from snap decisions to a sincere desire for blessing and unity.

Yes, unity—especially with those who are our brothers and sisters in Christ. According to Paul, this is not a unity that has to be *produced* but rather *preserved.* The phrase "to preserve" in Ephesians 4 verse 3 (NASB) comes from the Greek word *tereo,* which means "to guard like a watchman responsible for protecting a very important person." Think of it like the Secret Service personnel who wear the sharp looks and sunglasses around the president.

Does this mean that factions and conflicts in the church should be prevented at all costs? You'd better believe it. Wouldn't that be the conclusion you'd draw from "being diligent to preserve the unity of the Spirit in the bond of peace"? (4:3 NASB).

This doesn't mean we're all exactly alike, of course. It doesn't mean we'll always see totally eye to eye on every single item of discussion. But it does mean that our singular desire to lift up Christ and to be transformed into His likeness covers over all the other things that could threaten our unity and witness.

I'd even go so far as to say that if any two of us are not able to be like-minded in the Spirit, one or the other of us is not wanting what God wants. That's because this unity in the body is something God has already established. It's already there. It's not something we can manufacture, *but it is something we can break.* Therefore, we should be careful and watchful at the first sign of division. It's a signal that someone is tinkering with God's peace.

Oh, there's so much more to say about this, so much more the Bible teaches us about what grace looks like around the believer's shoulders.

But first, let's pause for this brief chapter break.

CHAPTER 6

Matching Outfits

[Looking Good in the
Garment of Christ]

Have you ever had on clothes that just didn't fit right?

About every time I teach on this subject of surrendering to Christ and putting His Word into practice, I do a little demonstration by looking around in the audience for someone who's much smaller than I am. Now this is not very hard to do because I'm a big guy, and there are a lot of folks who don't measure up to my body height and arm length. But as soon as I get the right person up next to me, I slip off my size 48, extra-long coat and ask him to put it on.

Well, you can imagine it. The baggy shoulders droop halfway down his arms, the pockets hang somewhere around his waist, and the sleeves either totally swallow his hands or perhaps leave the tiniest bit of fingertips to wiggle underneath the cuffs.

It's always pretty funny.

But, you know, it's not funny at all when you and I try to pretend we're wearing the garment of faith and righteousness, knowing deep down we're not anywhere near big enough to fill it out.

Hear me now, I'm writing this to myself just like I am to you. But I'm sure you can relate to what it's like being at home in the evening, tired and worn out from the day's work, belligerent and unresponsive, if not outright hostile toward your family . . . only to hear the phone ring.

Hmm. What a drastically different personality comes out of us when our public face and voice are suddenly called upon. The person on the other end of the line must wonder where we hide our wings and halo when we go out!

Am I right?

I mean, even though we may have spent most of Sunday morning being short and disgruntled with everyone in the house, who of us has ever scowled and brushed away the first handshake we were offered on our way into the church building? We would *never* show anything but our squeaky clean side once we opened the car door in the parking lot. But heaven help some of our "loved" ones who rode there with us!

Honestly, though, if we were truly submitting our hearts to Christ . . .

• Shouldn't our inside package fit the one we hold up for the outside world?

• Shouldn't the garment of Christ look and feel natural around our shoulders?

• Shouldn't there be a certain authenticity that everyone including us can spot?

This was Paul's point exactly in the last half of his letter to the Ephesians. And it's a point we can't afford to miss if we want to experience the living grace of Christ.

Inside the Dressing Room

At first blush—just thinking theologically here—it seems like our salvation should have taken care of this problem. The Scripture teaches us that our old man has "died" (doesn't it?), that our life is now "hidden with Christ in God" (Col. 3:3 NASB). Positionally and eternally, our sin nature has been rendered powerless by the redemptive act of Christ.

But while we are indeed new creatures in Him—with no demon in hell strong enough to snatch us from the hand of God—we are still able to choose (if we so desire) a lifestyle that reflects the old-man mind-set.

So when Paul told the Ephesians that they should take off their "former manner of life" (4:22 NASB), he wasn't declaring that they were still unsaved and needed deliverance from the penalty of sin. He was simply saying that as believers, they must continually "lay aside" the kinds of behaviors and attitudes that once kept them alienated from God, and to "put on the new man" (v. 24), the lifestyle that corresponds with Christian faith.

It's like taking off one piece of clothing and putting on another one. It's that basic.

We should know by now, however, Paul wasn't inferring that this is something we can do on our own. Christianity is never *outside in*. Unlike law-abiding, score-keeping, Bible-thumping religion, the wardrobe of the true believer is fashioned from the *inside out*. The garment of Christ is not something we put on to cover up what we don't want anyone else to see. Christ is the one who dresses us in His love and grace as He expresses His life from within us.

So don't go hunting for the garment of Christ in your closet. You won't find it there. Don't try sewing it on your own machine or manufacturing it on the assembly line of goals, commitments, and resolutions. Like everything else worthwhile in the Christian life, Christ's clothes become ours only as we bow down and surrender to Him.

If you don't like doing it this way, if you're self-confident enough to think you can put on Christlikeness anytime you want, just by using what's already in your wardrobe, then by all means go ahead. But I'm telling you from years of experience: you cannot reproduce godliness on your own.

Oh, I've seen people try. Not only that, I've done a good bit of trying myself. But although we can sometimes fake one or two *gifts* of the Spirit, accomplishing certain religious functions without the character to back them up, I've never seen anyone fake the *fruit* of the Spirit consistently in their lifestyles.

The garment is either there, fitting like it's supposed to, or it's not. And pretty soon, everybody can tell it, even if we're the last one to know or admit it.

So it's a fair question for me to ask you: *What clothes do you have on?* Are you wearing the garment of flesh or the garment of Christ?

And how do you know?

Trying on Clothes: Ephesians 4–6

From verse 25 of Ephesians 4 to around the middle of chapter 6, Paul did an awesome job of describing what these two garments look like. He showed us both the right way and the wrong way to appropriate the inner strengthening of Christ, either by letting our old man have his way or by letting Christ be preeminent in all things.

Paul introduced verse 25 with the word "therefore" (NASB), which tells us right away that he was laying down some conclusions based on the whole first part of Ephesians. (Whenever you see a "therefore" in Scripture, remember, always check to see what it's "there for.")

What follows is one of the most instructive sections in all the Bible when it comes to identifying the distinctives of Christian living. By showing us both the good and the bad—side by side—God continually gives us one opportunity after another to lift our areas of weakness before Him and ask Him to clothe us completely in His righteousness.

Truly, this is tailor-made for both teaching and learning.

So let's step up to the mirror and see how we look.

The Truth about Lying

Paul wasn't one to use the *Who Wants to Be a Millionaire* format, where you start off with the easy warm-up questions before they smack you with the hard topics. Instead, he came straight out of the chute with a one-two punch.

Right in the mouth.

"Since you put away lying, 'Speak the truth, each one to his neighbor,' because we are members of one another" (4:25).

Now most of us probably don't consider ourselves to be liars . . . at least not *too* bad. I remember, though, one particular day when I had come home for lunch and (as almost invariably happens) the telephone rang. It was for me. My wife cupped her hand over the receiver and whispered in my direction, "Are you here?"

"No!" I mouthed back in silence.

But not long after I pulled out of the driveway an hour later, my little daughter came up to Diana and said, "Mommy, isn't it a sin to lie?"

"Of course it is, dear."

"Then wasn't it lying to say that Daddy wasn't here when he really was?"

"Well . . . you see, honey . . . um . . ." (Those are hard arguments to win, aren't they?)

But let's be honest, lying can come pretty easy to us sometimes. In fact, it's *amazing* how quickly we'll lie when we're not living a life that's filled with the Spirit of God.

This goes back to the whole idea of Christ dressing us with righteousness from the inside out. One of our main motivations for trying to dress *ourselves* is to pro-tect our true identities. We want people to think of us in a certain way. So when a situation presents itself where someone might have the opportunity to catch on to us, we'll lie like a dog to meet our own needs and preserve our reputations.

I mean, what would have been wrong with my telling the person who called me at lunch, "We're just sitting down to eat. Would you mind if I called you back a little later?" But *n-o-o-o!* I didn't want someone to think I wouldn't drop whatever I was doing to spend time with him, even if he was the most ordinary person in the world. Nor did I want to look up from the hot ham-and-cheese sandwich I'd been looking forward to all morning.

Lying, it seemed, took care of me on both counts.

Isn't it tiring, though, having to come up with stories like that on the fly? Isn't it spiritually draining knowing that hypocrisy hovers so close to the surface in our lives?

And isn't lying—even in these seemingly trivial, understandable matters—the exact opposite of the way Jesus operated? As Peter wrote (quoting from Isaiah), "No deceit was found in His mouth" (1 Pet. 2:22). That's because Jesus didn't have any secrets to hide. He had no reason to beguile or mislead.

And this is the same Jesus who now lives in us. He's the only person we should really want people to see when they look at us and observe our behavior.

One of the greatest things about the grace-filled life is that it opens us up to be brutally transparent. My, how refreshing that is, not only to ourselves but also to other people who fully expect us to be fakes and phonies. It blows their minds to hear us being honest, not *glorying* in our mistakes but definitely not acting like we're above making a mess of things.

Listen, as I've said before in this book, nobody could tell me anything about my flesh that would shock me anymore. I know for a fact how rotten it is! I can tell you about one time, for example, when I was working on the computer in my hotel room, mistyped some letters on the keyboard while navigating the Internet, and accidentally found myself on a Web site preachers aren't supposed to visit.

But I stayed there for a couple of hours. Yes, I was fifty-something years old at the time. I knew full well what it meant to walk in spiritual victory. But I made a poor, conscious decision in the heat of the moment and gave my flesh permission to have its way for a while.

I wasn't happy that I had done it. I knew it was wrong. I confessed it to the Lord. And I figured that was the end of it.

Little did I know that personal computers leave online fingerprints everywhere we travel on them. And one day when I asked my secretary to take my computer for a while so she could help me figure out something on it, my secret suddenly came into the light.

She awkwardly mentioned it to me.

My heart thumped. My mind raced. The first answer that popped into my head was, "Why, *you* know I would never do something like that. Somebody who's borrowed my computer must have done this!"

But instead, pushing aside all the lies and excuses, I told her the truth. That's because the Lord has been kind enough to help me see that the Wayne-identity my flesh is so diligent about cloaking and disguising isn't really worth protecting after all. Unless he dresses me from the inside, I have nothing of value to present to the world.

I'll tell you what: no one gets more upset with me for sharing this story than the religious-minded folks in my world. It just goes totally against their grain for people to be up-front and honest about the rebellious part of their flesh.

Again, that's not to say we should ever take our sin lightly or shrug it off like it's no big deal. No way! But come on! It's time to get real. It's time for us to "speak the truth," to let Jesus so control our hearts that He even has control of our mouths—this "world of unrighteousness" that goes around disguised as our tongues (James 3:6).

When Christ is made at home in our hearts, we can finally be ourselves. We can be as forthcoming as He wants us to be, letting people see the underside of our lives without flinching, making excuses, or stalling them while we cram stuff under the sofa. When He dresses us in *His* garment, the gifts of truth and honesty are quickened within us.

And that's no lie.

Anger Management

Now for the second wave of Paul's one-two opening combination: "Be angry and do not sin. Don't let the sun go down on your anger" (Eph. 4:26).

Did he really say to "be angry"? Hey, I like that. I do it on the interstate all the time.

What Paul was really trying to show us, of course, is that there are two different kinds of anger: one that's pure and indignant, and one that's left to roll around long enough until it picks up a thick coating of sin.

Another way to classify these contrasts is to call them (1) the anger of God, and (2) the anger of man. Here's how I've learned to distinguish between them:

• The anger of God focuses on a *problem.*
• The anger of man focuses on a *person.*

Christ's coming to earth, I believe, was the perfect example of not only the love but also the anger of God in action. The problem at issue was human sin. And even though every single one of us was guilty, deserving the full brunt of His wrath, He turned His face to deal with the problem, not the people. He defeated sin because He loved us sinners.

God's anger is the kind that glows white-hot over injustice, over obstacles, over the pain in people's lives. Man's anger, on the other hand, is usually focused on revenge or winning an argument, the relentless pursuit of proving ourselves right. In fact, the *real* reasons for our anger are often lost in all the noise and tempter tantrums. That's when the target becomes our spouse, our parents, our kids, our boss, our neighbor, our employee, the guy who works on our car, or whoever's unlucky enough to cross our path at the time.

Whenever you have a particular person in the crosshairs of your anger, watch out! You're dealing with a rage that's both sinister and sinful.

Ask yourself this: if you're pretty sure you'd still be mad at that person—even if the problem was settled—that's the sign of an anger that's turned fleshly and personal.

But if you're not sure whether your anger is justified—if you can't tell the difference—I always advise people to confess it as sin anyway because most of our anger leans toward the anger of man. And we know "the anger of man does not achieve the righteousness of God" (James 1:20 NASB).

It's only with Christ inside us, filling our hearts with love and our minds with truth, that our anger toward others can melt into peace, and our hatred of sin can cause us to "be angry" for all the right reasons.

A Devil of a Chance

I heard one time that the devil was seen crying outside of a church. God walked by and asked him, "What's the matter? Why are you crying?" The devil answered, "You know I haven't bothered these people in six months, but they blame me for everything!"

Our problem isn't the devil, folks; our problem is the flesh.

But people look at Ephesians 4:27—the one that says, "Don't give the Devil an opportunity"—and they conclude that if we let him, Satan can somehow slip into our hearts and create havoc inside our lives.

That's ridiculous. As Christians we are filled so full of Christ, there's not even the narrowest back corner he can find to squeeze into. The holiness of God's Spirit inside us precludes us from becoming even a coffee break hangout for the devil. He's stuck outside with neither a key nor a crowbar.

And yet every time we pull on our old-man garments, we unwittingly become a ploy for the devil. When we robe ourselves in rebellion or religion, we do the devil's bidding, even though he may be nowhere around.

I'm telling you, the devil is not omnipresent. He cannot be every place at one time. We learn this from the first two chapters of Job, where even though Satan is seen "roaming through the earth," he's forced to rely on God to point out Job for him.

Oh, sure, the devil is powerful. Jesus called him the "ruler of the world." But He was also quick to add, "He has no power over Me" (John 14:30). And that includes us too, now that Christ has come to live in our hearts.

The context of Ephesians 4, remember, is the unity that exists in the body of Christ, a oneness we're commanded to "preserve" (v. 3 NASB) by letting God's Spirit flow through our attitudes and actions. It's clear, then, why Paul would want to bring the devil into this discussion, because "devil"—the Greek word *diabolos*—literally means "to cast through or divide."

The devil's desire, now that he's lost us for eternity, is to cause division in our relationships with others, to disrupt the unity that is such a compelling witness of Christ's presence in us. And when we give our flesh the chance to reign in our lives, when we flash back to the past and slip on the same clothes that characterize the lives of the lost, we give him an "opportunity" he doesn't even have to show up to capitalize on.

Give and Take

"The thief must no longer steal. Instead, he must do honest work with his own hands, so that he has something to share with anyone in need" (4:28).

It would be so easy to rush past this verse either without seeing *enough* of ourselves in there or seeing too *much*. What I mean is, few of us think of ourselves as thieves and robbers. For the most part, we're all hardworking people who, if anything, are guiltier of doing too much than too little. This verse almost doesn't seem to apply to us.

On the other hand, if all we see in this verse is a good piece of personal advice, we're forgetting (as we've seen) that this is a passage about Christian unity and relationships. Therefore, the whole point in not stealing from others, as well as the rationale for us to work hard, is so that we'll have "something to share" beyond the resources we need for ourselves and our families.

So this is a verse meant for all of us together. It's about giving and taking.

There are people in the body of Christ who are parasites. They come to visit us on Sunday mornings with one thing in mind: "What can this church do for me?" Whenever anyone asks me that question, I don't say this, but I think it: "You know what this church can do for you? We can recommend that you go find another one."

That's because these people are not seeking unity; they're seeking self. They're takers. They're stealers. They're depleters. Whenever they walk into a room, it feels like a good friend just left.

I'm not saying that some of these folks don't know a great deal of truth. I'm not saying they have no value in the church. But I wonder sometimes why they feel the need to seek their own fullness by emptying others. What are they hoping to accomplish by sucking the joy out of every conversation and encounter, constantly motivated by what's in it for them?

But don't we know people, too, who aren't like that at all? Don't we all know people who are givers? Sharers? Replenishers? Don't we all know brothers and sisters who are like a breath of fresh air in our lives, who leave us feeling blessed, inspired, and encouraged every time we see them?

People who are wearing Christ's garment don't go out to see how much they can take. They go out to give. Isn't that the way Jesus did it? "Even the Son of Man did not come to be served, but to serve, and to give His life—a ransom for many" (Mark 10:45).

Watch Your Language

"No rotten talk should come from your mouth, but only what is good for the building up of someone in need, in order to give grace to those who hear" (Eph. 4:29).

If you want to know whether someone really loves Jesus, just listen. You'll hear it. Over time their manner of speech will either confirm or convict them.

If you want to know whether *you're* wearing the garment of Christ today, listen to yourself. Hear what you're saying. See what you're contributing to conversations around the dinner table. Is it wholesome? Is it edifying? Is it giving "grace to those who hear"?

Some people tell me, "Well, Brother Wayne, there are times for talking straight, talking tough. Some occasions call for plain truth and hard words."

Boy, that is so true! I know it. But let me give you an example of what it's like to speak painful truth to someone without ripping them to shreds.

I played football in prep school as an end, a wide receiver. I was mainly used on third-down situations when we needed to make a play to keep the chains moving. Since I was one of the tallest guys on the team, I gave the quarterback a tall target for throwing to and was often able to get the first down.

We worked on this every day in practice. The coach would say, "I don't care how many yards we need for a first down, I want you to run your pattern ten yards deep. Put yourself so far in first-down territory that when the ball comes to you, you'll know you've gained enough yards."

All right. Fast forward to game time. Third down and long.

"Get in there, Barber!"

I went in, ran my pattern, jumped up between a pair of linebackers, and pulled the pass down. Only one problem: instead of going ten yards, I had only gone nine and a half.

"Barber!" my coached screamed as I trotted to the sidelines.

I knew what was coming. My coach had played professional ball and was tough as nails. He was about six-eight and wore a size 56 extra-long coat. Huge man! He grabbed me by the shoulder pads—all 225 pounds of me—and lifted me right off the ground.

"How many times do I have to tell you to run your pattern ten yards deep?" he growled (among other things) into my face mask. Sufficiently vented, he hurled me back to level ground where I hoped I might find a hole waiting for me, big enough to crawl in.

While slumping back toward the bench, however, I heard him hollering my name again: "Hey, Barber!"

"Sir?"

I looked back, not knowing what was coming next.

"Beautiful catch," he said, almost smiling.

What he had said to me through spit and fury a few minutes before had been hard truth, uncomfortable to hear, I promise you. But by leaving me with a word of encouragement, he made me want to get back out there and play again.

That's what it means to edify someone, even when the truth hurts.

Paul, we know, had some tough things to say to the church in Corinth. But because he was wearing the garment of Christ, he could blister their backsides while honestly saying, "I'm not writing this to shame you, but to warn you as my dear children" (1 Cor. 4:14). He loved them too much to speak rudely to them, yet he also loved them enough not to hold back from saying what they needed to hear.

If we're not careful—if we're trying to survive spiritually in our own strength, using nothing more than window dressing—our talk will inevitably turn "rotten." Some translations of verse 29 use words like "unwholesome," "corrupt," or "foul."

But I sort of like the word "rotten." That just kind of says it all.

Have you ever been driving down the road and caught a whiff of skunk in your car? What does everybody turn to each other and say when that happens? "Pyooo! That stinks!"

I wish sometimes, whenever anybody called to share a piece of gossip or hearsay with me, I'd holler back into the mouthpiece, "Pyooo! *Please* don't make me listen to any more of that! I can't stand the smell of it!"

Wouldn't that expose divisive talk for what it is? Wouldn't that put the brakes on anybody using you for a partner in gossip? Wouldn't you be doing your part to preserve the unity of the church?

Look at it this way: "If anyone thinks he is religious, without controlling his tongue but deceiving his heart, his religion is useless" (James 1:26).

You'll know Christ has *you* when He's got you by the tongue.

Show Me Some Love

All of this basically boils back down to love. This is the overriding fruit that bubbles forth when Jesus is made at home in our hearts, when His garment is working its way through us from the inside out.

For example, when His love is emanating from us, we'll have no desire to do anything that would "grieve God's Holy Spirit" (Eph. 4:30).

Grieve is a love word. It expresses the sorrow felt by someone who's been mistreated or abused, the kind of sorrow we should want to avoid causing Him at all costs. It's also a *present tense* word, which carries the idea that this grieving of the Holy Spirit is an ongoing habit of ours, that we're routinely taking advantage of and disappointing the God who's redeemed us.

We've all been there, haven't we? We've all gone through stretches where we brought much more sadness than joy to the Spirit's eyes. That's because we were either trying to please Him by our own righteousness, or we were flaunting His presence by rebelling against Him to His face.

This is serious business. The Spirit grieves easily.

Yet I believe, too, that we can receive this doctrine as an unduly heavy burden. Some people are always concerned that they've done something irreparable against the Holy Spirit. They're skittish that maybe they've stepped on His last nerve.

I truly believe, however, that grieving Him has a lot more to do with our *attitudes* than it does with our *actions*. We usually know when our hearts are cold toward the Spirit's influence, don't we? Therefore, our response at these times—instead of wallowing in guilt for a week and a half—should be to fall on our knees before Him, surrender every selfish thought and motive, and ask Him to have His way again in our hearts.

We love Him too much to wish for anything less.

When we do, we'll notice a marked absence of some of the flesh's most telling signs, found in Ephesians 4:31. Things like . . .

Bitterness. This is sort of like having acid in your stomach that you'd love to spew on someone else, but chances are, it's going to eat you up first before you can get it out of your system. It's like the ulcer I had one time. I went to the doctor to find out what was causing my pain, to see what I needed to do about my diet to alleviate it. He said to me, "Wayne, this is not about what you're *eating*; it's about what's eating *you*." Storing up bitterness is how our flesh feeds on itself.

Wrath. Unlike bitterness, this is that type of explosive anger that builds and builds until it finally erupts. Have you ever had one of those days where everything was going wrong? People were being ugly to you, everything was taking three times longer than it should, and nothing you'd planned had turned out like you wanted. All it would take now is for one person to cross you, and she might get a whole day's worth of frustration dumped in her lap. That's wrath. And it's only avoidable through surrender.

Clamor. This word means "loud speaking or shouting." This is when you cross the line, becoming obnoxious, mean, ugly, insulting.

Slander. The word in Greek is *blasphemia,* which gives us an idea for how serious this sin is. It means "to speak against" or "to tear down someone's character."

Malice. More than anything, it's this deep-seated hatred—the opposite of love—that truly drives all the others. Just as the love of Christ motivates us to godliness and gentleness, the simmering hatred that seethes inside our flesh will regularly act up in ways that are mean, cruel, and short-tempered toward others.

Yet when the love of Christ is captivating us, transforming us, He'll grow some dramatically different traits within us. You'll find these in verse 32:

Kindness. This is the idea of being useful to one another, serving one another.

Compassion. This means having a tenderhearted sensitivity to people's needs.

Forgiveness. It's a divine forgetfulness, not being able to remember a wrong.

This one is big. I've known people who couldn't quote John 3:16, but they could remember December 3, 1987, when I offended them by not coming to see them in the hospital.

Christ, though, can give you a divine eraser to smudge out any record of an offense done to you. You'll remember being hurt, perhaps, but you won't remember why. It's beautiful when Jesus allows you to walk in that kind of freedom and forgetfulness.

Super Strength

Throughout all of Ephesians 5 and the first nine verses of chapter 6, Paul continued to show us the difference between the garment of flesh and the garment of Christ. Always it was in reference to our relationships—husband and wife, parent and child, brother and sister.

At last Paul came to what we now know as Ephesians 6:10, where he decided to wrap up the body of his letter: "Finally, be strong in the Lord and in the strength of His might," followed by his well-known description of the armor of God.

Many people, without taking into account the context of this passage, consider this to be a whole new teaching, as though Paul was totally changing the subject, suddenly speaking about spiritual warfare without regard to what he'd been saying all along.

No, no. The armor of chapter 6 is the same as the garment of chapter 4. He was continuing to talk about the same thing—the incredible love and power that exudes from within and surrounds from without when Jesus is living His life through us.

He's the warrior, not us. And that ought to make us feel "strong in the Lord."

Back when my son, Steven, was in high school, we started making it an annual ritual to attend one of the postseason tournaments in college basketball. One in particular that I remember was a trip we took to Atlanta to see the NCAA Southern Regional.

Now some of you would rather take a beating, I'm sure, than endure the first day of this marathon event: four straight basketball games, back to back.

For us, it was awesome. The popcorn, the hot dogs. You just sit there all day, yelling your lungs out. Great fun!

But after sitting through the first three games, knowing that the last one wouldn't be tipping off until nearly ten o'clock, *even I* wouldn't have put up a fight if my son and his buddy had said they'd just as soon skip it and go back to the hotel. After all, the final contest of the night was between the second seed—the Kansas Jayhawks—and the fifteenth seed, some school called . . .

Robert Morris?

Now, in the years since then, Robert Morris University has made quite a name for itself in basketball. I've learned that it's a little private school up in Pittsburgh. But I can tell you that on this particular night in Atlanta, of the ninety-five hundred people still sitting in the stands at ten o'clock, only about five of them had ever even *heard* of Robert Morris.

Pretty soon they introduced the Kansas starters one at a time, each of them running off the bench to the roar of the crowd, the beat of the pep band, and the delight of the cheerleaders.

And then came the Robert Morris squad. No tubas, no trumpets, no hoopla. They didn't even have on warm-up suits, just their game uniforms. Their shoes didn't match one another's. It looked like they'd picked these guys up off the playground on their way to the arena.

This was a game between the haves and the have-nots if I'd ever seen one. *Should we stay? Should we go? What do you guys want to do?*

We decided to stay and pull for old Robert Morris.

Kansas won the jump ball to start the game, drove down and fed it to their big boy in the middle, who proceeded to sky for a slam dunk. But before he could stuff it into the basket, one of those Robert Morris boys leaped from the foul line and blocked the dunk from behind. It was incredible!

The ball bounced off the backboard and right into the hands of a Robert Morris player, who turned and dribbled down to the other end, where he shot and missed everything. He was so nervous. Actually, both teams were looking kind of sloppy at first, trying to get in sync, dealing with the disparity in the competition.

But all of that changed a few minutes later.

Robert Morris had the ball. One of their big boys worked himself open in the middle, spun around the tallest of the Kansas giants, took it to the hole, and thundered home a dunk that just about pulled down that whole backboard. WOCKA, WOCKA, WOCKA, the thing rattled.

Silence erupted into bedlam. Suddenly it seemed like *everybody* was on the underdog's bandwagon. And the more we yelled, the better they played. By halftime, those upstart Colonials from Robert Morris were neck and neck with the Jayhawks of Kansas.

During the break the Kansas cheerleaders rushed back out on the floor, trying to get their fans back into the game. The band played. The crowd swayed. It seemed like everyone was returning to their senses.

But then those tiny cheerleaders from Robert Morris took the floor. One of them pulled out a CD player, laid the public-address microphone right in front of the speaker, and blew the wax out of our ears with an old-time rendition of "Rock Around the Clock." It was unreal. You couldn't hear yourself clapping.

Then once the music ended, everything got quiet. One little, lone cheerleader padded out to the middle of the floor, facing the stands opposite us. She cupped her hands to her mouth and, trying to get a response from the fans, yelled out, "RAHHH-bert!"

Nobody knew what to do. So she tried it again, louder this time.

"RAHHH-bert!"

Finally, a few sharp minds on the other side realized she was trying to get a cheer going. They shouted back, "RAHHH-bert!"

Then she turned to face our side of the gym, and yelled out, "MORRR-iss!"

We hollered back, "MORRR-iss!"

Pretty soon, the whole place was in a rhythmic uproar, the gym throbbing like a beating heart, pulsating to the sound of "RAHHH-bert! MORRR-iss! RAHHH-bert! MORRR-iss!"

I'm telling you, when the Kansas team emerged from the locker room, the crowd booed them. The whole tide of emotion had changed. From top to bottom, side to side, this place was wanting a win for ol' Robert Morris.

Sure enough, the game went back and forth, nip and tuck, the Robert Morris five playing out of their heads, keeping it close all the way to the end. As it often happens, however, the valiant effort of the underdog came up just short.

But I wondered with my son and his friend, as we left the arena around midnight, how lopsided a loss Robert Morris might have endured if the crowd hadn't been on their side in such force. I said, "You know, guys, this is one of the greatest illustrations of the Christian life I've ever seen."

(They looked at me like I was nuts. I kept talking anyway.)

"Let me ask you a question: Didn't the team do better when the crowd found joy in what they did? The joy of the crowd became their strength."

Of course, this reminds me of that verse from Nehemiah, where he told the people rebuilding the walls, "The joy of the LORD is your strength" (Neh. 8:10 NASB). In other words, when we know we're pleasing Him, saying yes to Him, surrendering to Him—when we can sense His strength and power flowing through us, overwhelming us, transforming us—this fuels our desire to keep on trusting Him. Like the writer of Hebrews said, we become "*trained* to distinguish good and evil*" (Heb. 5:14). We grow into godliness as we experience Christ producing it in us.

Jesus is knitting his garment in you from the inside out. No, you won't wear it perfectly every time. You'll decide every now and then that you like your old clothes a little better. But if all you ever do is just *think* about letting Christ lead you, making plans to surrender to God somewhere down the line, you'll never get to try on His garment at all.

Living the grace life only happens when we yield our lives by faith, and let God do it . . . in the middle of an average day, during moments when we think we can't possibly make it, at times when we're tempted to resort to our old man.

Want some new clothes to go with your Christian life? Then let Jesus sew as you go.

Remember Robert Morris.

CHAPTER 7

It's the Only Way to Fly

[Still Surrendering after All These Years]

Some things never change.

The years roll by, your children grow up and have their own children, generations pass off the scene, and yet some things never change.

When I was about twelve years old, I told my mom that I wished I'd never been born. Even at the time I knew it was a dumb thing to say. But we had been in an argument—one of those where she knew she was right, I knew I was wrong, but I wasn't about to give in.

And boy, when I said that, it made her so mad. She got all red in the face, her eyes began to water, her nose began to run. And the madder she got, the madder I got. The louder she raised her voice, the louder I raised mine in return.

Finally I said to her, "Why don't you just go ahead and hit me?"

Dumb again.

Most mothers (if they'd been willing to take you up on it at all) wouldn't have done anything more than just slap you in the face or something.

Not my mama. She hauled off and hit me right between the eyes.

There I was, thinking my nose was broken. There she was, staring at her clenched fist, surprised at the right hook she never knew she had.

Before it was all over, though, we were both standing there laughing in the kitchen. "Wayne," she said, "when are you ever going to learn?" And it dawned on me: if there was to be any peace in our home, it was going to have to start with me. I had to be the one who did the giving in, submitting to my parents' authority. It's been this way for children for as long as there have been families and fusses.

Some things just never change.

It's the same way with the Scriptures. The things we read in the Bible never change. They're true in the Old Testament. They're true in the New Testament. And they're still true today, just as they will be ten years from now, twenty years from now, a hundred years from now.

That's why, when I teach on Ephesians (as I've been doing in the last few chapters), I always like to follow it up by going back to the Book of Joshua. That's because, even in that ancient historical account from many centuries ago, God was already approaching His people in the same way, instructing them in the same truths He would show Paul hundreds of years later, the same truths He's still showing us today.

Then as now, it's all about surrender. This is what unlocks the door to everything that's ours in Christ Jesus. The Christian life is never a matter of getting more; it's always a matter of appropriating what we already have.

Surrender, of course, is nothing more than the white flag. It means saying to God, "I give up. I'm through fighting with You. I'm going to let You dictate the terms and call the shots. Everywhere I've resisted You before in the past, I now relent. I give up. I give in."

And guess what: when you *give* in, you *enter* in. (Just ask Joshua.)

Some things never change.

Twin Tracks

Before we get any further, I need to say this: one of the most important things to remember when you're studying the Old Testament is that you're traveling a two-lane street and you need to keep your eyes on both of them at the same time.

It's kind of like my experience one afternoon in Dilley, Texas. I was involved in a speaking engagement there, and the car I had been loaned during my visit (believe it or not) was carrying expired Nevada plates on it. The drive from where I was staying to where I was speaking was about twenty miles. And the whole time I was looking around in all directions, scared to death I'd be caught and pulled over at any minute.

Sure enough, not long into my trip, a state trooper eased in behind me on the interstate. When I'd speed up, he'd speed up. When I'd slow down, he'd slow down. Before long, he had maneuvered his car into the left lane, and he stayed hinged to one side of my rear bumper for fifteen miles or more.

Well, you know what that's like. With one eye I was watching the lane in front of me—the lane I was doing my best to operate my vehicle in—following every rule and regulation in the driver's manual. With my other eye, however, I was constantly checking my mirrors, heavily aware of what was going on in the opposite lane.

Reading the Old Testament is a lot like that.

• On one hand, God is dealing specifically with His people, Israel.

• On the other, He's incorporating principles that apply to everyone.

And all of this is happening simultaneously.

You just have to be careful. I've heard people over-spiritualize various passages from the Old Testament, claiming every single promise God made to Israel as a promise to us. But that's not always the case. Some of the activities of God we read about in the Old Testament were specifically linked to the situation at hand. We can't just automatically extrapolate them to fit any current occasion or opportunity we choose. We shouldn't read *ourselves* into everything that happens there.

However, some eternal principle usually runs alongside the events chronicled in Israel's history. And we are welcomed and invited to let God reveal these truths to us.

We just need to remain discerning as we study.

For example, when the Lord told Joshua, "Prepare to cross over the Jordan to the land I am giving the

Israelites" (Josh. 1:2), He wasn't saying that we could command the creek beside our house to part so we could cross without getting our feet wet. Nor was He guaranteeing that we could pray for a parking place to open up nearer the door so we wouldn't have to walk so far.

But there's still a truth inside. For where the people of promise had been given a *land,* we saints of God throughout the ages have been given a *life.* And the same principles God initiated with His people through the wilderness lands and war zones of the ancient Near East still apply to the lives we lead on this side of civilization.

Catching Up with Joshua

OK. Just to get ourselves on the same page, let's make sure we remember where things stand at the beginning of the Book of Joshua.

Moses, of course—who had been Israel's leader and guide for an entire generation—was dead. But some time before, God had instructed him to "take Joshua, son of Nun, a man who has the Spirit in him, and lay your hands on him," conferring onto Joshua a measure of authority in Israel's affairs (Num. 27:18). Moses was getting old, and change was on the horizon. Forty years of aimless wandering in the desert was nearing an end. Joshua was to be God's man to lead the people into the land of promise.

So in the very first chapter, we get to listen in on a private address from Jehovah God to Joshua—His new man on duty—where the Lord rallies him to begin occupying the land (pay attention now) which *"I am giving"* to Israel (Joshua 1:2).

Oh, that really bothered me when I first read that!

I'll tell you why. Let me take you back to Numbers 33:53, where the Lord told Moses, "You are to take possession of the land and settle in it because *I have given* you the land to possess."

Let me also take you back to Numbers 27:12, where the Lord had earlier said to Moses, "Go up this mountain of the Abarim range and see the land that *I have given* the Israelites."

Let me even take you all the way back to Genesis 15:18, where the Lord said to Abram—before he was even Abraham—"To your descendents *I have given* this land" (NASB). Past tense. "I have given." There's no other interpretation but this: the land was already theirs.

So why, my mind questioned, would God talk to Joshua about "the land *I am giving* the Israelites" if it was the same land He had already given them?

Want to muddy it up a little more? Look at the very next verse. God, continuing to address Joshua, now seems to revert back to His old stance by saying, "*I have given* you every place where the sole of your foot treads, just as I promised Moses."

So which one is it? Had God *already given* the land to His people of promise, even from a date farther back than His covenant with Abraham? Or was He *just now* giving it to them in Joshua's day? Is this nothing more than my trying to split hairs and word pairs? Or is there really something here we need to know?

I believe God shows us the reason for this variation in verb forms by using one innocent little phrase in verse 3: "the sole of your foot" (or as the Hebrew word for *sole* more specifically means, a "bare foot").

OK, barefoot. What does that make you think of, Old Testament-wise? Probably the same as me: the burning bush. We all know the story. Moses saw a bush that was burning but wasn't burning up. He went to investigate. And as soon as God knew He'd attracted Moses' full attention, the first thing He told him was, "Take your sandals off your feet, for the place where you are standing is holy ground" (Exod. 3:5).

There would also be an event a short time later in Joshua's life, just before the battle of Jericho, when the "commander of the Lord's army" appeared to him with a drawn sword in his hand. Joshua, after dropping facedown in worship, was told by this divine visitor (most believe it was Jesus—including me), "Remove the sandals from your feet, for the place where you are standing is holy" (Josh. 5:15).

Something about being barefoot before God was obviously (in Old Testament times) the proper response to walking on "holy ground." And it's the same way in the New Testament, just as it is today.

Surrender: God's All Time Plan

I believe the Lord was saying to Joshua, "Every place that the bare part of your foot touches— every place that you walk in humble obedience to Me, recognizing that I'm the one who really matters here— is ground you can begin to occupy. Certainly all of the land is yours. I've already given it to you. But the only portion of it you can actually live in is the part you approach surrendered, submitted—the part you walk through with your spiritual shoes off."

This is the same land, remember, that was every inch as much an inheritance to the previous generation of Israelites as it was to Joshua's. But the story from

Exodus through Deuteronomy is one example after another of how rebellious, ungrateful, disobedient, and obstinate these people were—*stiff-necked,* to use a really good King James word. As a result, they never entered into the land God had given them, the land that was rightfully theirs.

But here at the beginning of the Book of Joshua, God was reminding Israel's newly appointed leader that the land was still there for the enjoying if they would only be willing to walk into it humbly, trustingly, worshipfully.

Barefoot.

Oh, how we need to hear this! Ask yourself if it doesn't square with what we've learned in Ephesians. Paul said to that first-century church, "Look at what all you have in Christ!" He wanted them to see that the problem wasn't their lack of spiritual resources but their failure to appropriate them.

And still today we are only able to enter into the abundance of Christ by this measure: how willing are we to walk with a surrendered heart?

In those areas of our lives where we lay down our right to be in control—those tracts of land where we yield our will to the Father—we experience His provision by the bucketful. But wherever we dig our heels in, demanding that the property be deeded to us so we can do with it as we please, we find ourselves mired in failure and frustration, looking for peace and joy everywhere, but never able to find it.

We don't even have to look far in the Book of Joshua to see this coming true:

Why was Israel able to wipe its feet on Jericho's doorstep? Because they trusted God to give them victory, even if it meant walking passively around the city for a week and firing nothing more than a trumpet blast as a weapon. If that's what God said, that's what they did.

But why was Israel soon routed by a much smaller force in Ai? Because they thought they could whip them with their eyes closed, because in the glow of an easy win over a much tougher foe, they saw no need to bother God with something they could obviously handle themselves.

One battle was won by surrender, and another was lost by smugness.

Listen to how the psalmist captured this truth, recalling the days of Israel's grumbling and grousing in the wilderness, when they refused to let God lead them in any way other than one that met with their approval:

> Today if you hear His voice: "Do not harden your
> hearts as at Meribah, as on that day at Massah in the
> wilderness where your fathers tested Me; they tried
> Me, though they had seen what I did. For 40 years
> I was disgusted with that generation; I said, 'They
> are a people whose hearts go astray; they do not know
> My ways.' So I swore in My anger, 'They will not
> enter My rest.'" (Ps. 95:7b–11)

The reason they could never possess the land wasn't primarily because they *disobeyed*. In fact, there were times along the way when they seemed to be obeying, when with their mouths (at least) they were saying all the right things and acting in the short-term as if they were serious about doing things God's way. Their real problem, though, was the condition of their hearts, because before obedience can ever happen, *surrender* must take the place of surliness and stubbornness.

This is what Jesus tried to tell the Pharisees all the time. Good gracious, they had the obedience part down, but they didn't understand that *true* obedience only comes through surrender.

You see it, too, in the life of Simon Peter. Wouldn't you say he gave up his nets and followed Jesus *long* before he gave up Simon Peter?

Yes, we can give things up but still hold ourselves back. We can obey the legal letter of what God says but still have no life. The only way we can ever truly enter in is to submit to Him every step of the way. "For the person who has entered His rest has rested from his own works, just as God did from His. Let us then make every effort to enter that rest, so that no one will fall into the same pattern of disobedience" (Heb. 4:10–11).

Blessing follows obedience. And obedience follows surrender.

Some things never change.

Security: God's All Time Promise

Sure enough, God's plan from the beginning of time was that surrender would always result in success. Men and women who have stubbornly demanded their own way have always found the going rough, while those who throughout time have willingly submitted to God's power and purposes have discovered something supernatural to their lives.

And what goes for God's *plan* also goes for His *promise*. His word to us continues to hold true in all of its depth and color, year after year, age after age, life after precious life.

Take this promise, for example. "No one will be able to stand against you as long as you live. I will be with you, just as I was with Moses. I will not leave you or forsake you" (Josh. 1:5).

Now this would have been an outright lie if God had said, "No one will ever *try* to stand against you." Every one of us knows certain people who have a real knack (knowingly or unknowingly) for attempting to steal our joy, test our patience, and totally wreck our spiritual equilibrium. But "trying" is a long way from "being able to." And though people can do their best to snatch peace and perspective from our lives, the only way they can succeed at it is if we *choose* to let them win.

That's God's promise. Yesterday, today, forever.

The question is: if we really believe it, how do we walk in it?

I'll have to admit that for the most part, I probably don't. I've got a Ph.D. in how to do things my own way instead of God's way. So do most people. But I know one time for sure when I saw this promise work in big, dramatic fashion.

When I was pastoring in Chattanooga, our church really began to grow as we started preaching the Word of God and unashamedly lifting up Christ. The truth went out, and the people poured in. It was quite humbling, quite amazing. But as our church began to attract a fair share of notice and recognition in the community, I discovered to my surprise that the church of Satan had a major following in the Chattanooga and North Georgia area.

Up until then I had no idea. I really didn't even know there was any such thing as a "church" of Satan, people who actually get together to worship and pray to him. It seemed like such a ridiculous notion to me, I'd just never given it much thought.

This all changed, however, when I began receiving letters addressed to me (always spelling my name wrong), threatening to harm our church and kill my family if we didn't stop what we were doing. I guess they figured that just by throwing Satan's name around, they were going to convince us to close up shop and start selling off Sunday school space.

It got worse.

At the time our church was conducting multiple worship services on Sunday, with up to 150 people regularly spilling out into the foyer at each one of them. It wasn't uncommon for me to have to walk over and around people just to get to the platform.

In the midst of this exciting, expansive season in our church's life, the Satan worshippers decided to dispatch about twelve people to our services each Sunday, planting them in different places all over the building. And they would pray out loud even while I was praying, reading Scripture, or making announcements. No matter what we were doing as part of our worship, the Satanists were there, praying curses on us and inciting our people to fear.

The ushers would come up to me from time to time, asking me what I wanted to do. Should we throw them out? Should we lock the doors? Should we call the police?

No way! We just decided to pay them no mind. We continued to magnify, exalt, and lift up the name of Jesus, even when we had to do it above the noise of their devilish prayers.

And in about six weeks, they left, never to return.

Yes, they had *tried* to stand against us. They had done their best to scare us into sniveling submission. But they were *not able* to stand against the people of God, not when our total focus and attention was on the reigning King of glory, not when we were taking every step by faith.

It worked for Joshua. It worked for Paul. It worked for our little church in Chattanooga. It'll work for you.

The Lord God is the only source of our joy. He is the exclusive home of peace and rest and hope and security. Every time we go out looking for these things, believing we can find them without needing to keep our eyes fixed on Christ, they will never turn up. If we put our confidence in other people, expecting them to meet our needs, we'll be disappointed every time. If we look to our husband or wife to be our sole supply of confidence and acceptance, we'll end up lacking in both departments.

Oh, sure, God will use many people to bless and encourage us, but he alone is the giver of life and spiritual stamina. If we try to borrow it from others, or manufacture it ourselves, or hoard it from those who want to steal it away from us, we'll turn up empty-handed and disillusioned.

Our strength will come from God, or we will have no strength at all.

An old fellow came stalking across the sanctuary one night after I'd finished a weekend conference at a particular church. It had already been a tough few days. It seemed like everything I had tried to say had fallen flat. Every bit of humor I'd tried to inject had landed without even a ripple. Just nothing. No response. Totally dead.

And to top things off, here he came. I could tell from his walk, his expression, and his buzz-cut determination that this had all the earmarks of a knockout punch.

"Preacher," he scowled, once he got me within range, "I've been doing rescue mission work for twenty years. And I don't need anybody coming in here trying to entertain me."

"Well, I'm sorry, sir, if I offended you. I certainly didn't mean . . ."

Before I could finish my apologetic response, he had already turned away—only to think of something else he needed to get off his chest and whirl back to face me. "Another thing: If you can't say everything you need to say in twenty minutes, after that you're just showing off."

His final blow dealt, he wheeled around again to walk away.

Then something came over me. I wouldn't call it pure holiness. I reached over his back, grabbed him by the collar, and spun him around to where I was standing. I won't tell you the first thing that came to mind while I was quickly deciding what to say or do next. But in a spiritually charged split second, the Lord poured cold water on my boiling temper and forced out of me something I never expected.

"Sir, would you pray for me?" I asked.

"Wh-what do you mean?" he shot back.

"I mean: would you pray for me?"

"What for?" he snarled.

"Because God's obviously not finished with me yet, and I need His help if I'm ever going to be all He needs me to be."

Whoosh! Now the cool water of Christian fellow-ship was melting *both* of our hard hearts. And this guy who had wanted nothing more than to steal my joy had been neutralized by the power of God, protecting us both from robbing each other.

It's tough, I'm telling you. Our flesh dies hard. We're tempted to want to protect ourselves, to fight back, to handle our own dirty work. But God's plan is for us to surrender. And His promise is that nothing can "stand against" us when we do.

So if we're not living in what God says is already ours, why not?

Scripture: God's All Time Priority

Do you ever feel weak and worn out? Is fear a reg-ular visitor in your thoughts and motives, in your actions and reactions? Are you amazed sometimes at how spiri-tually spineless you can be?

You're certainly not alone.

I even have an idea that Joshua, for all his reputa-tion as a gutsy, heroic warrior, still had a scared streak that ran down his back. Underneath his "as for me and my house" assurance, I believe he dealt mightily with the insecurity of following in Moses' humongous footsteps.

Here's why I think so. In the last half of God's open-ing message to Joshua (1:6–9), the Lord had to remind him *three times* to "be strong and courageous." This tells me that apparently boldness and bravery weren't just oozing from every pore of Joshua's body. His natural man—like ours—didn't always wake up feeling ready to take on the world.

But that's OK. In fact, that's good. Successful Christians are not those who grit their teeth and go do it. The essence of walking with God means putting our full confidence in Him. It means coming to the place in our lives where we realize that all the strength is His, not ours.

Oh, sure, we can sometimes think we're bullet-proof. We can get all worked up in a worship service and head out the doors with a big "strong and courageous" message ringing in our ears. We think *nothing* could snuff out this head of steam we've got! But you know what? We're lucky if we make it till evening before the power fades back to normal—that is, if the church parking lot doesn't take care of it first! Strength and courage simply don't grow naturally in these hearts of ours.

But they can. And here's how: The Lord said to Joshua that He would make strength and courage available to him if Joshua would "carefully observe the whole instruction My servant Moses commanded you. Do not turn from it to the right or the left, so that you will have success wherever you go" (v. 7).

The word for "success," by the way, really means "to act wisely" or "to make correct decisions." It's certainly not limited to financial or material success; it speaks more of the inner character and integrity of a person.

God went on: "This book of instruction must not depart from your mouth; you are to recite it day and night, so that you may carefully observe everything written in it. For then you will prosper and succeed in whatever you do" (v. 8).

Stay in the holy Word of God, Joshua, and I will show you how to take the land I've already given you.

How foolish it is to act big and strong without it.

I know people who say they have faith, but what some of them really have is presumption. Without basing their opinions on one shred of Scripture, they convince themselves that God is going to do some particular thing for them. Well, He may or He may not. It depends on whether it's in keeping with His holy will. But just because someone *believes* hard enough that God is going to act in a certain way doesn't paint God into a corner where He will violate His character, which is revealed to us in the Bible.

If we're not in the *Word* of God, we have no idea how to determine the *will* of God.

Remember how the psalmist put it? "How happy is the man who does not follow the advice of the wicked, or take the path of sinners, or join a group of mockers! Instead, his delight is in the LORD's instruction, and he meditates on it day and night" (Ps. 1:1–2).

What a great word *meditate* is! When I first looked it up in the Hebrew dictionaries, I discovered that one of the examples that best describes the idea of meditating is a cow chewing its cud.

When I saw that, I knew exactly what they were talking about! We once lived in a house in the country that backed up to a cow pasture, and I used to watch the cows all the time over the fence. They were so interestingly funny to me, strangely peaceful in their slow, lumbering way.

You don't have to keep your eye on a bunch of cows for long before you'll see them working that cud in their mouths, lapping those extra-long tongues of theirs up and down and around until you just want to burst out laughing. They're just hilarious to me.

Cows (you may or may not know) have four stom-achs. So whenever they've finally ground up their grass or hay and swallowed it down for the first time, all they have to do to keep enjoying it (are you ready?) is just to burp it up again. Back and forth this goes on all day long—eating, swallowing, burping, then eating some more—keeping all four of those big, fat stomachs involved in digesting the same patch of grass.

Now I don't know if this gastric word picture does anything for you (like, perhaps, making you want to throw up), but I hope it at least helps you see what God instructs us to do with His Word. We get up in the morning, and we take it in—reading it, thinking about it, praying over it, asking for understanding. Then all day long, whenever we need it, God brings it back to mind. He draws His Word up from within us—since we've been faithful to put it there to begin with—and now we receive it in a new way, fresh and alive and ready to learn from.

This is what Jesus was talking about when He said, "The Counselor, the Holy Spirit . . . will teach you all things and remind you of everything I have told you" (John 14:26). When you need it, He'll bring it back to your remembrance so you can dwell on it again, lay it atop a certain set of circumstances, or share it with someone who needs to hear God's truth.

That's the beautiful, powerful result of meditating on the words of Scripture . . . day and night, night and day. You'll recognize the fact that God is instructing you because you're used to how He speaks. You're accus-tomed to hearing His voice, over and over, in the Bible.

My mother has been dead for many years. Her mean right hook aside, I'd give just about anything to visit with her again, to drive over and spend the day with her, to hear her laugh and feel her embrace. I wonder sometimes what it would be like if the phone were to ring, and when I picked it up, she would be on the line.

"Wayne?" she'd say.

"Mom!" I'd answer back in surprise.

"How'd you know it was me, son? I've been gone so many years."

"Aw, Mom, I'd know your voice anywhere." Why? Because it had been so much a part of my life, such a customary ingredient in so many days.

Getting into God's Word is much the same way. The more time you spend in it, the more you learn about what matters most to Him, the more easily you can spot His fingerprints on a certain situation or solution.

And with the confidence that comes from knowing He's working through you, teaching you, leading you into the life He's promised you, the more you'll experience His strength and courage bubbling up inside you.

It's the only way to fly.

Come In Where It's Warm

I heard the story of an eighteen-year-old boy who was just about at that age where he was wanting to sprout his wings and try life on his own. He was getting tired of having to submit to his parents' authority on everything, and he was impatiently waiting for the time when he could leave home.

One cold, wintry night he was sitting in the family den, silently sulking. For anyone else it would have been the picture of perfect peace. Succulent aromas floated from the kitchen where his mom was cooking the evening's dinner. Light glanced off the wood paneling and reflected its gleam in the windows.

Yet as the snow and the temperatures were falling outside, the fire was likewise starting to dim a little in the fireplace. The boy's father, sitting with his feet up, watching football on television, turned to his son and said, "Why don't you get up and put another log on the fire?"

Fed up and feeling every ounce of rebellious ambition flaring up inside him, the boy leapt to his feet and exclaimed, "No way! Not any more! I'm outta here!" He bounded up the stairs, crammed his stuff into a bag, threw on his jacket, stormed to the door, and slammed his way into a new future.

"I'm sick of things never changing around here!" he grumbled to himself, clomping through the crusty snow that was still falling around him. "I'm gonna start doing things *my* way for a change."

After walking about 150 yards, however, the first real bite of raw wind began to freeze his cheeks and hands. His muscles tightened. His body shivered. And almost as a reflex, he turned to look back to the home he had just left.

Through the window he could see the honeyed glow of the den burning warm against the gray sky and snow-white landscape. With the night air cutting through his too-thin jacket, he longed again for the radiating comfort of his father's fire roaring above the hearth.

"What in the world am I doing?" the boy said to himself, spinning on his heels and running back to the front door he had so recently shut behind him. Knocking rapidly, he could hear the creak of a chair inside as his father rose and walked to the door. Opening it, his father motioned for his son to come in, took his snow-wet coat off his shoulders, and patted him warmly on the back. "Your mom will have dinner ready in a minute. Run upstairs and get into some warm clothes. It's good to have you back, son."

The boy did as he was told, returned several minutes later in clean socks and pajamas, and plopped down beside his dad. They talked for a few minutes, the boy shyly apologizing for being so rude and stubborn. The kind father, of course—understanding what can well up inside the human heart—forgave him effortlessly. As they smiled at each other, the son sensed the love and respect for his dad rekindling in his heart.

Then suddenly, the conversation grew quiet. The father settled back into his chair and eyed the embers burning low under the mantelpiece.

"Son," he said, "why don't you get up and put another log on the fire?"

Some things just never change.

• Surrender will always be the path to obedience and blessing.

• Spiritual security will always be the birthright of the born again.

• The Scripture will always be a prerequisite for Christian courage.

Some things never change. And we should thank God for it every day.

CHAPTER 8

The Ultimate Open-Book Test

[Can a Person Ever Look
Forward to Finals?]

We've covered a lot of ground in this book. We've talked
about:

* *The weakness of the flesh,* the sheer impossibility
that we can ever do anything good on our own.

* *The completeness of our salvation,* the righteousness of Christ that not only forgave us but also sustains us.

* *The frustration of the law,* the do-more attitude
that can rouse nothing else inside us except rebellion or
self-righteousness.

• *The riches of God's blessing,* already given in full supply to those who've believed in Him for new life.

• *And the necessity of surrender,* the only way to experience the day-by-day joy and confidence of following Christ.

As we saw from the beginning,

I can't—God never said I could.

He can—and He always said He would.

There's no getting around it. Success in the Christian life never comes from working ourselves into obedience. Self-righteousness stinks just as bad in a believer's life as it does in an unbeliever's. So we can stop playing games and skirting the issue. We can quit trying to compare and outperform. We can abandon our failed attempts at earning God's approval through self-willed sacrifice and obligation.

We are here on this earth simply for God to work through. Our goal in life should be for Christ to blaze forth His righteousness through our hearts and hands, our eyes and smiles, all submitted to His will.

Nothing else matters, nothing else lasts, except what Jesus does through us.

That's why I believe the best way to wrap up this discussion of grace and surrender is by looking at ultimate realities, end results. One reason many of us have struggled so in our Christian life, trying desperately to appear righteous and check off our list of duties, is because we've limited ourselves to the temporary and inconsequential. We're still worried about what others will think about us. We're controlled by a desire to get things done . . . fast. We rarely see past next weekend or a month from tomorrow.

Perhaps, though—when you think about it—the most unique, extraordinary element about being a Christian is that we have a real future, a forever promise that eclipses every earthbound attempt to confine us to twenty-four-hour days or even eighty-five-year lifetimes.

We are people of eternity. Not just then but right now.

So I want to take you—in our last chapter together— to a passage of Scripture that I think addresses this issue well: the third chapter of 1 Corinthians. It's a teaching that is often misconstrued with negative connotations. Some people nervously fear its message and dread its implications. *We shouldn't* because Christ's purpose in judging His people is not to strip us naked or embarrass us in front of the whole entourage of heaven. I can promise you that.

The truth is, *we* are not going to be judged at all when Jesus gathers His saints around the throne. *We* were judged at the cross and found worthy of redemption through Christ's blood, based solely on the Father's grace and mercy.

We're in.

But do you want to know how wonderful our Lord and Savior is? He has decided not only to assure us eternity with Him in a new heaven and a new earth. As if that weren't enough, He has even chosen to *reward* us for the way we appropriated His righteousness through our daily lives, to celebrate the power we allowed Him to display in us. Imagine that!

Now He doesn't have to do this. No one has twisted His arm or advised Him that this might be a good motivational tool, sort of like an incentive bonus for reaching our performance goals. This is simply the result of His own good pleasure, intended to honor and glorify the work He was able to accomplish through His surrendered servants.

Jesus is not taking things away. He's just adding on to an already heaping pile of blessings.

What could possibly be negative about that?

And what more reason do we need for living our lives in humble submission to Him, now that we have absolute certainty that His life in us is all that matters?

Problem Children

The church in Corinth was a mess. As a matter of fact, Paul—over the course of two lengthy letters to this particular congregation—never once had a good thing to say about them. The only positive quality he was able to find in them was their *potential,* what he knew they *could* become if they would ever surrender to Christ.

He said, "I always thank my God for you because of God's grace given to you in Christ Jesus, that by Him you were made rich in everything—in all speaking and all knowledge . . . so that you do not lack any spiritual gift" (1 Cor. 1:4–5, 7). These people had everything in the world they could possibly need and nothing good to show for it.

It's not as though they could blame it on the preaching. Their first pastor had been Paul himself, followed by Apollos, a man described in Scripture as most learned and eloquent. Even Simon Peter had spent time teaching and training the people there. These three spiritual giants had invested so much of themselves into this bunch of believers, and yet little of it seemed to be getting through. You can almost hear the weariness and frustration in Paul's voice as he wrote, "It has been reported to me about you, my brothers, by members of Chloe's household, that there are quarrels among you" (1 Cor. 1:11).

The word Paul used for "quarrel" here doesn't imply that they were just having a little disagreement. This wasn't a minor peeve or a difference of opinion. Apparently, their quarrel was ripping apart the body of Christ in this influential Greek city. The people who were standing on one side of the issue weren't budging an inch, and the ones on the other were sticking just as stubbornly to their side. To make things worse, it wasn't just a *few* who were poisoning the unity for everybody. Paul addressed his complaint to "each of you"—every living being who had aligned himself with the church there.

This was an absolute, scratch-your-eyes-out impasse.

Over what? you ask. To tell you the truth, their sticking point was no less petty than most of the ones we quibble over in the church today. In fact, there are plenty of modern-day congregations dealing with the exact same issue Paul was trying to drum out of Corinth two thousand years ago!

They had aligned themselves into four camps:

• *Paul's people*—the ones who were there at the beginning, when Paul was in charge.

• *Apollos's people*—those who favored and were attached to his style of leadership.

• *Peter's people*—the ones who felt superior because of their allegiance to the apostle.

• *Christ's people*—the group who didn't think anybody was quite as saved as they were.

You've seen this happen in churches, I'm sure. A new pastor comes in to replace the previous one, and people snidely draw themselves up into groups. One bunch favors the old guy and won't give the new man a chance. Those who've come along *after* the fact—as well as those who'd been counting the days till the former pastor finally left—stake out their position as opponents of the old guard. They like the new fellow and his new ways best, and they don't mind telling you about it!

Now none of these men—Paul, Apollos, Peter— none of them were the least bit interested in organizing their own fan clubs. Paul, in fact, was adamant about it! He was disgustedly glad that he hadn't baptized anybody in Corinth except maybe for a couple of people (vv. 14–17). He didn't want anybody acting like they were more official just because Paul had been the one to perform the act.

But people do this anyway. It's our natural tendency. We get attached to the ones who have fed us so faithfully and so well. We don't mean to take it too far. We don't mean to get to the point where we feel more allied with a pastor or church leader or Bible study teacher than we are with Christ. But we often do . . . to the detriment of ourselves and our churches.

But don't you see the flesh at work in all this? Whenever we get our eyes on ourselves or on other people, the flesh will feed off that fuel for days.

Paul once said to the church in Rome, "I tell everyone among you not to think of himself more highly than he should think" (Rom. 12:3). And in his first letter to the Corinthians, I think he was taking this same principle one step further. Not only do *we* not belong on a pedestal; neither does anyone else.

And this (among many other things) was the problem at Corinth.

The Whole Life Policy

"Wayne, why in tarnation are you spending so much time on this? What do the problems in Corinth really have to do with us living a life of grace and surrender?"

I just want you to see that we have only two choices in life—either to attach ourselves to the flesh or to attach ourselves to Christ. And whatever choice we make, everything else in our lives will be impacted by it.

Look at the Corinthians. They obviously gave their flesh ample opportunity to roam. Paul just came out and told them: "I fed you milk, not solid food, because you were not yet able to receive it. In fact, you are *still* not able, because you are still *fleshly*" (1 Cor. 3:2–3).

As a result of this condition, we read about a man in their church who was living with his mother (probably his stepmother), and nobody had the courage to call him on it. The man himself wasn't willing to curb his passions, and the church was more afraid of dealing with an awkward situation than in practicing redemptive discipline. Fearful of appearing harsh and confrontational, they simply caved in to their habit of maintaining comfort over integrity. They even figured it was pretty big of them to be so tolerant.

That's the flesh at work.

We also know that the believers in Corinth had gotten in the habit of suing one another at the drop of a hat. Instead of relenting their own agendas and surrendering their personal rights, they were dragging their problems before the pagan courts and hashing out their troubles for the whole world to see. Men and women who were destined to walk on streets of gold were haggling with one another over money matters. What a wonderful witness they were displaying in the public square!

But that's what happens when the flesh is in charge.

When they had the option of either exercising their own freedoms or protecting their weaker brother's tender sensibilities, they chose their own rights every time.

Instead of honoring Christ in their Lord Supper observances, they gorged their appetites on the bread and wine and whatever else their friends brought for dinner.

Although God had bestowed them with gifts to serve and build up one another, they used their individual ministries for their own amazement in order to boost their spiritual superiorities.

And it's the same way with us. When we start with the flesh, we're guaranteed to reap its wicked rewards in every aspect of our lives. If it doesn't show itself in outright rebellion, it'll assume a religious form that's every bit as distasteful in the eyes of God.

But if we will begin each day surrendering our wills to Christ's purposes, if we will present ourselves *to* Him rather than putting on a show *for* Him, the results of His righteousness will trickle through us from head to toe. And before we know it, His life flowing through us will become the norm, not the exception.

This is not something you can talk yourself into. Neither is it something you can set like an oven timer and walk away from it. Having Christ continually operating in you is a reality you must *live* to believe.

And, oh, how He wants to take us there . . . if we'll let Him!

An Individual Test

When Jesus saved us, he poured a new "foundation" in our lives (1 Cor. 3:11). The solid rock of His grace became the basis not only for our salvation but for everything of worth that we'll ever do the rest of our lives.

So from that moment on, you and I became builders. But we "must be careful" (v. 10) how we build on this foundation. We have two sets of building materials to choose from (v. 12):

• "Gold, silver, costly stones"—the valuables that Jesus produces in us.

• "Wood, hay, or straw"—the cheap imitations we pile up ourselves.

Two different choices. Two different results.

While we're here, of course, it's hard to tell the two apart. If you hold them up to the light just right, wood, hay, and straw can give off a glint of gold. But a day is coming when "each one's work will become obvious, for the day will disclose it" (v. 13).

Now here's where people get jumpy. They equate this "day" of 1 Corinthians 3 with the "day of the Lord," that oft-mentioned moment of judgment when unbelievers will feel the full brunt of God's righteous anger and be flung into the lake of fire. Oh, sure, this fact should chill us for the sake of our unsaved friends and family members who are facing this grim future as long as they reject the name of Jesus. But we who have been bought with the blood of Christ have nothing to fear from this judgment. We are already included in the Lamb's book of life and in the grateful throng of the redeemed.

But Paul talked about another "day"—the "day of Christ Jesus"—when God's people will be declared "pure and blameless" (Phil. 1:10), when we will be eternally assured that we did not "run in vain or labor for nothing" (Phil. 2:16).

This is a day we should be looking forward to, when our citizenship with Christ will be confirmed and celebrated. As Paul said, "He who started a good work in you will carry it on to completion until the day of Christ Jesus" (Phil. 1:6).

So don't fear this "day" we're discussing in 1 Corinthians 3. This is a day of blessing and reward, of hopes fulfilled, of Christ appearing as the ultimate answer to our prayers. Whatever His revealing fire burns away from us on that day will not destroy us.

But, oh, what joy—perhaps even surprise—when that fire leaves us holding "gold, silver, costly stones," the incredible results of a life surrendered to God. Suddenly, everything He's accomplished through our lives will be disclosed for His glory and our amazement:

- People He's ministered to . . . through us.
- Work He's accomplished . . . through us.
- Disciplines He's sparked . . . through us.
- Hearts He's encouraged . . . through us.
- Dreams He's rekindled . . . through us.
- Patience He's granted . . . through us.
- Love He's given . . . through us.

I can't wait!

Please, now, don't misinterpret this to mean that we're going to be saved by our good works. No, don't think that all these little acts of service we've performed will each be assigned its own allotment of brownie points.

Notice that the Bible says, "Each one's *work* will become obvious" (1 Cor. 3:13). Not *works* plural but *work* singular. This is so important. The Scripture doesn't use words lightly or without intent, so we need to consider what makes our *work* different from our *works*.

I believe this means that our daily actions of trust and surrender are creating for us a body of *work* that is set to be revealed at the last day.

We certainly haven't been perfectly submitted to Christ every moment of our lives. We know that we have a whole lot of lost time and opportunity that's already under the bridge. But God's desire for that "day" of fire and revelation is not to nitpick and finger point. His plan is to uncover the prevailing motives of our lives, to make known the totality of who we are and how intent our heart has been on honoring Him.

If you don't think you've allowed Christ to produce much gold or silver in your life so far, don't worry that he's already been in the editing room, piecing together a bunch of damaging clips that will embarrass you in front of your friends and family. Look, you can change all of that right now! You can throw off the meaningless memories of rebellion and indulgence, of apathy and indifference, of self-styled religion and look-at-me, aren't-I-something spiritual pride. You can put today in the hands of God—this very evening or afternoon—and watch your life turn golden right before your eyes.

The story of your life's work is still waiting to be written. And you can change the closing page between now and the end of your life as Christ changes you into a man or woman totally sold out and surrendered to His will.

When you stand before Him individually—not in your wife's or husband's shadow, not under your pastor's umbrella of influence but simply between you and

Him—you can know the sweet experience of being honored by Christ for your "work" as a believer.

Yes, you! How cool is that!

A Revealing Test

"Each one's work will become obvious, for the day will disclose it, because it will be revealed by fire" (1 Cor. 3:13). The New American Standard Bible translates it, "Each man's work will become evident; for the day will show it."

Let's take some of these words one at a time and see what they have to teach us.

Evident is the Greek word *phaneros,* which means "to cause something to be manifest, to be made so visible that everyone can see it." This carries the idea of a brilliant light shining on something, the kind of light that leaves nothing hidden.

Thinking about bright lights always reminds me of the South Carolina swamps where I used to do a lot of deer hunting. It gets darker than usual down there, it seems. And after you've seen rattlesnakes that stretch half a highway long with your own eyes or black panthers that slink their sleek bodies across your path, you want to be sure you know where your next footstep is going to take you.

In the mornings, when we'd be working our way into the woods and up to our tree stands, I didn't feel the need to use much more than a penlight to illuminate my way. But when we were coming back out of the swamps in the lengthening shadows of night, I didn't want any surprises! That's why I went out and bought myself an industrial strength flashlight, one of those superheavy jobs that takes about five big batteries to work it.

So, buddy, when I came out of the deep woods, people knew it was Wayne coming!

Man, I loved that flashlight. I'd climb out of my stand, sling my gun over my shoulder (with the chamber loaded, of course, in case I came across any unexpected night stalkers). Then I'd reach down and click the power switch on that flashlight. *Whoom!* Pitch blackness lit up like sunrise. The squirrels came out. The birds started singing. They thought they'd overslept. It was just awesome!

And in much the same way on that great day of Christ Jesus, the light of His presence is going to peel back the shadows. Nothing will be hidden. No excuses will work. No need to make up a good story.

Everything will become clearly "evident" and "obvious."

The next little phrase to discuss from verse 13 is "show it," which comes from the double-o word *deloo,* meaning "to declare or inform." And what does the Bible say is going to do the showing, the disclosing? *"The day* will show it."

I don't know about you (and I certainly wouldn't fuss with you about it one way or the other), but I believe that "day" is when Christ comes for His church.

This seems to be the same day Paul was talking about in 1 Thessalonians 4. The young Christians over in Thessalonica, you may recall, were concerned about what would happen to the dead bodies of their believing loved ones. They knew that the *spirits* of these brothers and sisters had gone to be with Jesus. But what about their physical *bodies* that had been buried in the ground?

Paul encouraged them by saying, "Since we believe that Jesus died and rose again, in the same way God will bring with Him those who have fallen asleep through Jesus" (1 Thess. 4:14). What Jesus will be bringing with Him, of course, are the *spirits* of the departed church, believers who have died in Christ.

"For the Lord Himself will descend from heaven with a shout, with the archangel's voice, and with the trumpet of God, and the dead in Christ will rise first" (v. 16). This could be nothing other than their physical bodies, resurrected from their lifeless state to be joined with their eternal spirits. "Then we who are still alive will be caught up together with them in the clouds to meet the Lord in the air; and so we will always be with the Lord" (v. 17).

And all of this will happen "in a moment, in the twinkling of an eye, at the last trumpet" (1 Cor. 15:52).

I've had a lot of skeptics come up to me and say, "Wayne, what about a body that was blown apart in a foxhole by a grenade? What about a body that was disfigured in a horrible murder or an airplane crash?"

Or try this one: "What about a body that was cremated? How is *that* body going to be raised from the earth?"

Paul Harvey told the story of a woman who, while vacuuming the house one day, accidentally knocked over and broke the urn containing her husband's cremated remains. Not knowing where to put him, she scurried through the kitchen cabinets until she came across an empty sugar bowl. She figured he'd be safe in there until the next day when she could go out and get a new urn to replace the broken one. When her daughter stopped by later in the afternoon, however, with an armful of groceries for her mom, she poured a two-pound sack of sugar into the same jar her father had been resting in.

"How, Wayne, is God going to resurrect a body like that?"

I even heard of a situation in Reno, Nevada, where some teenagers broke into a house, turned over an urn that was on the mantelpiece, and—thinking the powdery substance inside was cocaine—snorted a cremated body right up their nose!

"How, Wayne, is God going to resurrect a body like that?"

Well, I don't have the slightest idea. But I'll tell you what: the same God who stepped out on nothing and spoke all things into existence is big and strong and smart enough to do what He says He'll do. And if that poor soul who was stirred by the spoonful into a cup of coffee was a believer in Jesus, then I'm telling you, he's going to show up on the day of Christ in a resurrected body. The Bible declares it!

And as for me, I truly believe that this resurrection "day" is the one Paul was referring to in 1 Corinthians 3 —the great day of Christ Jesus when we are going to be rewarded for our willingness to live for Him, when the illuminating presence of Christ is going to provide information about us we didn't know before.

"The day will show it."

Finally, Paul says that this information will be "revealed" by fire. This is the Greek word *apokalupto,* which means "to uncover or unveil." It's like a curtain coming up, bringing something unseen into view.

This is a reality of life we all need to deal with. "For nothing is concealed that won't be revealed, and nothing hidden that won't be made known and come to light" (Luke 8:17). We're fools if we hide our heads in the sand and pretend this isn't the case.

But although our flesh approaches this fact with fear and dread, scared to death of being unmasked, only God in His grace can turn this potential nightmare into a spiritual desire. When we are renewed in our devotion to Christ, living to love Him and bring Him honor, making our lives accessible and accommodating to His Spirit's presence, He relieves us from the fear of this revelation. Because of Him, you can rejoice in the fact that "your Father who sees in secret will reward you" (Matt. 6:4).

Now maybe you don't believe this. But if you just don't feel like you can live without working to accommodate the law and the flesh, then get used to having this lingering dread hanging over your head. Go to sleep every night not knowing when the other shoe is going to drop. Cover your tracks and hope for the best.

But I assure you, peace and rest can be yours if you want it. Your future can be stripped of fear and phobic apprehension. Every one of us who believes in Christ for salvation can live with perfect confidence in Him, unafraid of what might be made known about us on the last day.

How? Because it won't actually be *us* on display on the day of Christ, but *His work* accomplished through us. All we need to do is surrender, presenting our bodies and minds to the Lord instead of offering them to sin, letting God live through us what is pleasing to Him.

A Quality Test

Last but not least, not only will this day of reward be an *individual* test, as well as a *revealing* test, but it will also be a *quality* test. As Paul said, "The fire will test the quality of each one's work" (1 Cor. 3:13).

As soon as I say that, I know the first thing most of us see in our heads is the image of a red-faced preacher, jabbing his finger at us, warning us that "GAWD is going to get you one day! He's going to take all your sins, pile them up in front of you, and leave you totally exposed for who you really are."

Good grief, I hope these preachers feel better after they get that off their chests because this is not the feeling we should be left with after reading these verses. Yes, our work is going to be revealed by fire. The Scripture is clear about that. But remember that our God is a "consuming" fire (Heb. 12:29). Whatever part of us is "wood, hay, or straw" is going to be burned into nothing, obliterated from view . . . not left to humiliate us.

The biblical term "test," by the way, comes from the Greek word *dokimazo*. We find the same word over in 1 Peter 1:7, where this identical "fire" imagery is used— not to frighten us but to encourage us! Peter told his readers that the reason they had been enduring such a difficult time in life was "so that the proof of your faith, being more precious than gold which is perishable, even though *tested* by fire, may be found to result in praise and glory and honor at the revelation of Jesus Christ."

This "test" is a *good* thing! Wanting God to receive "praise and glory and honor" from choosing to work through us should make us want to dance around the house! His intention is not to embarrass us but to reward us, to thank us, to bless us!

Yet our natural tendency is to read fear into this process. We run right past the part that says, "If anyone's work that he has built survives, he will receive a reward" (1 Cor. 3:14), thinking Paul must be talking only about Billy Graham or Martin Luther or the guy who runs the homeless shelter downtown. *Paul couldn't possibly be talking about us, could he?*

No, we usually see a lot more of ourselves in the verse that reads, "If anyone's work is burned up, it will be lost, but he will be saved; yet it will be like an escape through fire" (v. 15). Many of us feel as though we might be one of those who walks into heaven with our britches burned, black smudges on our face, our hair standing on end and smelling of smoke.

But that's the attitude of the flesh talking. That's the feeling of someone who hasn't fully gotten the good works out of his salvation system.

The truth is, it's impossible for a person to be saved and see no spiritual fruit growing as a result. To believe otherwise goes against every biblical teaching on Christ's redemption there is. Those whom God has chosen and received to Himself will follow Him—not perfectly—but with a lifetime's worth of desire to yield more of themselves to Christ. To be a Christian and not want to see our lives colored in his gold and silver qualities is a contradiction in terms.

But even if it weren't—even if it were possible to claim Christ's life yet never want anything else to do with Him—even then Christ's righteousness would be enough to save us.

News flash: *It's all that's saving us right now!*

The point of verse 15 is that there's not enough goodness even in the skin of our teeth to make us acceptable to God. But because of Christ's righteousness in us, we are still salvation worthy.

So don't be afraid of standing barefooted before the Lord, exposed to His revealing fire, an open book of past choices and poor efforts. Begin today by surrendering your own plans into God's powerful arms, and you will begin experiencing a freedom that will make you look forward to forever.

Only the flesh can make us more concerned about ourselves than about our Savior. When that wonderful day comes, you'll be so excited about seeing Him, you won't even be thinking about what He sees in you.

Grace to You

I could go on forever (although you'll probably be glad to know I won't). But I do hope and pray that the Lord has spoken to you through His Word as we've traveled these important ideas together. The reality that we are not only saved by grace but are sustained by it day after day is one that should fill our lives with sweet relief toward God and open arms to one another.

The Bible is so clear in saying that our own goodness is much worse than we perceive it to be, hopelessly deficient in earning us anything close to acceptance in God's eyes. Yet in laying ourselves openhanded on the altar of His will, in giving up any hope of earning our good reputations, in scorning every artificial attempt at appearing more holy than we are, we find Christ manifesting His character through us.

We find patience and gentleness growing where there used to be nothing but clenched teeth. We find peace and joy flowing where doubt, despair, and who-cares skepticism used to clog the Spirit's freedom. We find love bubbling up in hearts that used to only show itself if people met our requirements, if we felt like they deserved it.

We find ourselves living in grace.

I'll tell you the truth, I'm not all the way there yet. I don't suppose, actually, that I'll ever get there this side of heaven. None of us will.

But why should that keep us from surrendering ourselves afresh with each sunrise, recognizing our cotton-pickin' flesh for the scoundrel it is, and choosing to live our next few waking hours in humble reliance upon Christ's righteousness?

Who knows what He might do through us if we'd let Him?

Who knows what kind of gold, silver, and costly stones we might find assembled around our feet on that great day of final victory, fire, and testing?

There's only one way to find out.

Want to?

Grace at Work

[A Special Word to Pastors and Church Leaders]

The message of grace is something every believer needs to hear, simply because so many people are needlessly burdened down with guilt and exhausting expectations.

But we know, too, that Christian ministers can be just as much in need of grace as anybody else.

For one thing we are routinely forced to endure the criticism, suspicion, and ridicule of those we're simply trying to love. Yet sometimes we quit loving. And the grace we want from others becomes lost on us as well. In fact, we are often rightly accused of being the very ones who place the harshest, most debilitating demands on others.

That's why I want to take a moment to share a personal word with you at the end of this book, those of you
who labor every day to care for, preach to, and serve the
people of God. These truths about grace have been broken
open on me in the context of being a pastor and Bible
teacher for many years—just like you—so I fully understand how easy these things can be to preach . . . and how
hard they are to live.

That's what has made this journey into grace a bitter-
sweet one for me. If I could have made the trip without carrying this *flesh* around with me all the time, it
would have been *all* sweet! But most of the lessons God
has taught me in this area have come through my own
flat-out failures, a level of hypocrisy that should have
shocked me long before it did.

And yet, in God's grace—there it is again, the living
grace of God!—He has given me multiple chances to
repent and return to Him, even after I've gotten myself
hung up again in legalism and appearances. Boy, do I still
have a long way to go! But the Lord has shown me clearly
that this message of grace can only be *learned* by being
lived. The yielding of our will to His Word is not a mental exercise but a daily experience, an ongoing choosing,
a muscle, a reflex we can only develop by using.

In reality, the only alternative to letting Christ live
in and through us is stubbornness and contempt for His
will to grow inside of us. And believe me, it's not hard for
these character deficiencies to find the kind of soil they
like—even in us ministers of the gospel.

Today's Christian ministry—as it has been throughout the centuries, I'm sure—is overrun with pastors and
church leaders who come across as if they have it all

together while they're secretly living another life behind the mask. I'm not talking necessarily about gross, hideous, closet sins, although none of us are immune from even the vilest offenses. Primarily, though, I'm talking about the equally wicked sins (in God's eyes) of spiritual coldness, pride, ambition, superiority, and personal laziness about heeding, desiring, and being daily transformed by the Word of God.

People are looking for pastors who are real, pastors who admit that living for Christ is hard on them too, pastors who have quit underestimating the distrustful, deceitful influence of their flesh, who wouldn't give you two hoots for their own integrity outside of what Jesus is fashioning inside them.

It took a long time for me to realize this. I used to think my flesh wasn't so bad. And even when it acted up, I felt sure I could get it back in shape with the right amount of exercise, good attitudes, and sacrifice.

But brother, you can forget that! A pastor's flesh is no holier and righteous than anybody else's. And don't we get to find this out in new ways every single day (not to mention in old, all-too familiar ways, as well). I get sick of it, and I know you do too.

I don't know how many times, for example, I've had to ask my wife to forgive me for the hateful and callous way I've treated her. Even though I have the sweetest, most capable, most tenderhearted, caring wife in the whole world, many times I have broken her spirit by a look, a quick answer, an exasperated expression. Oh, how painful to think of it!

Same thing with those who've served before and are serving with me now on the church staff. Like you,

I've had to go to them on numerous occasions, asking forgiveness for the careless way I spoke to them, or the lack of support or defense I was willing to provide them.

I've even had to stand up in front of the entire congregation at certain times and beg their pardon for failing them, for being far less than godly before them, for allowing my flesh to control my life.

So with your indulgence—and hopefully for your and my benefit together—I want to think through a few matters of particular importance with you, areas where grace is most desperately needed in our lives as pastors and ministers.

The Church: The Making of Our Ministry

Roy Hession, author of *The Calvary Road*—that great Christian book that has had such an impact on me and so many others—told me years ago that "the church is my school of brokenness."

I'm sure at the time I didn't have the good sense even to realize what he was saying. But I have certainly learned over the years how right he was.

As hard as it may be sometimes for us to believe or accept, it is the goodness of God that places us in situations that stretch us out of measure—stretch us to the point where we either have to depend on Him or sink under the strain. If He never put us there (and we know good and well we'd never choose to go there on our own), we wouldn't be able to live the message of grace we so want others to understand.

Again, grace isn't learned until it's lived.

- Grace isn't learned until deacons want to dominate us with the sheer weight of their own self-importance and sense of entitlement.
- Grace isn't learned until a member of our staff has become so territorial he can no longer see the big picture, filtering everything through how it affects his own ministry area.
- Grace isn't learned until we've been criticized for everything from the hymn choices to the service order, from the size of our car to the size of our salary . . . "just for working on Sunday!"

Our flesh screams out that these are rank injustices, the rantings and ravings of small-minded idiots. What we don't tend to realize, though—unless God has our hearts, our full surrender to His will—is that these are all tools in His hand, chipping away the knotty, no-good pieces of our old man that are clouding people's view of Christ in our lives.

Listen, it hurts to yield to Christ, especially when we're determined that we're in the right and we want so badly to make sure everybody knows it. The pain that our flesh feels when we deny its noisy tantrums is hard for us to ignore. But a defeated ego is essential in order for us to become vessels Christ can use and work through.

Oh, we can preach, and give, and minister, and come off looking like a million bucks a good bit of the time and still be operating with a flesh that's in full control. Far too much of what I've called "ministry" over the years has been nothing more than pure flesh seeking recognition. But that self-styled part of me and my work will burn to ashes at the judgment seat of Christ. That part of me that measures everything by results and numbers, that takes pride in myself and my accomplishments while shamefully giving phony, token credit to God, is destined for destruction.

Join me in draining pride from your life. Be more transparent every day about who you are apart from Christ's grace and empowerment. Never forget that we haven't been sent to our churches for *them* and *their* sakes as much as they have been put here for us, placed into our lives and ministries by a loving God, intent on driving us to the end of ourselves . . . and into his strong, waiting arms.

The church is indeed our "school of brokenness."

People: Opportunities Disguised as Problems

I remember thinking to myself, once I began to understand that Christ truly lived in me, *nothing could stop me now!* The sweet revelation that I was free of having to perform for God's approval, free of having to earn His love brought me alive in a way I'd never experienced before. It was a dynamic, dramatic rush of relief and renewal.

But man, was I ever in for a surprise!

All it took was one critical phone call, and my Christ-centered confidence could unravel like sweatsocks that had suddenly sprung their elastic. I couldn't believe how easy it still was to topple me with a word, to knock me over with a feather.

But that's when God slowly began to teach me—not slowly because of Him but because of me—that the message of *Living Grace* can never be seen as a concept to be understood, a way of thinking we adopt. It must be lived out, situation by testing situation.

For example, I will never be convinced otherwise that there isn't a school for *mean women* somewhere. And one of the primary places they dispatch them upon graduation is to whatever church I happen to be in at the time. I've held several pastorates over the years, and I declare, I've had alumni at every single place.

I'm kidding, of course (a little). But I'll say this: Those people who've been the most obnoxious in the way they've treated and talked to me (men very much included) have been the ones the Lord knew I needed in my life. Through their snippiness and pettiness, I have been painted a depressing picture of who I am apart from Christ. It has made me understand that "He in me" is the only hope I have. And through some of the hardest of these relationships, I have seen God work amazing acts of unity and reconciliation.

I have seen grace grow in places where the flesh could do no more than gripe.

So, yes, when e-mails become drive-by shootings, and people who claim to be Christian can take potshots at your spirit through the hurtful things they say and do *to* you and *about* you—it's hard. The pastorate is definitely not the easiest place to walk by the Spirit, especially when you have to deal up close and personal with the unvarnished flesh of other people.

Just speaking for myself, I can tell you that God created me six-feet, seven-inches tall, and I weigh around 260 pounds. By some measurements, those kind of numbers would indicate strength and power, if not at least a legitimate need to go on the Atkins diet.

When it comes to dealing with my fleshly first impulses, though, my substantial height and weight don't give me an ounce of help. But, oh, just to have five minutes behind the building with some of those people who give me such grief—it would tickle the daylights out of my human nature.

We have to be careful. We have to be willing to be misunderstood. We have to let Jesus' humility and love overpower the big, hulking lug our flesh would like to be.

It's not just *mean* people who are a problem, of course. I served with a lady once who just loved to talk. She was indeed a dear, precious person, but there was no such thing as a conversation with her that didn't last at least twenty minutes. I could call just to tell her I was going to be late coming in, and before I knew it, the morning was starting to slip away and she was telling me over the phone how to make German chocolate cake. It was unreal!

One day she came into my office at a particularly busy time, and I knew I was in for at least a forty-five minute dialogue if I didn't head it off early on. My flesh was really bristling at the intrusion, and I was about to say something when I caught a glimpse of a picture on the wall, just over her shoulder from where I was sitting. It was a picture of Jesus. And at that moment I was reminded that this woman had a need, and that this moment was a divine interruption. I silently said *yes* to Christ, and He calmed my irritated nerves. I listened. We talked. And the joy He gave me during that hour was greater by far than any benefit my counsel or direction could possibly have been to her.

People are not our problem, dear friend. They are our opportunity.

Never allow people—and the careless way they may treat you—stop you from letting Christ live through you. Try to take each situation one at a time, and just say *yes* to Christ in the middle of it. In that moment He will manifest Himself through you. And because of His power, expressed through your submitted soul, people will no longer see *you* as much as they see *Him*. It's a beautiful thing, even if it's not an easy thing.

Truly conflict is the proving ground of *Living Grace*. Christ in us produces His love through us, so that no one can long refute that it's coming from Him.

So when those who have the gift of dissension drop in out of nowhere to ruin your day, immediately say to Christ, "I can't handle this alone, Lord. You know that. But I ask You to do through me whatever You want to do."

By saying *yes* to Him, we say no to our flesh, and we bless our brothers and sisters.

Competition: The Danger of Comparison Ministry

One other point I want to encourage you about is the "big church" thing.

We live in a day when people think if it's big, it must be of God. But I believe the term *megachurch* has done more to bring glory to the flesh than just about anything we've ever introduced into our church vocabulary. It's not only poisoned our thinking about true success, but it's broken the hearts of pastors in small churches who feel like something's wrong with them for not preaching with PowerPoint and a high-tech screen.

Although ministry can happen in so many various ways—and we should all be grace-filled enough to let our prejudices die on the altar—one thing must remain steady in our steering mechanisms: ministry is not something we *achieve* for God; it is something we *receive* from God.

So let the size of what He has given you . . . satisfy you.

Everything about the way I used to do ministry has had to change—and continues to change—as this message of *Living Grace* sets me free. For one thing, I've just totally quit worrying about measurable results. Results are none of our business. Why worry about matters that only Christ can do anything about? Our responsibility is simply to walk with Him in His Word, yield to the prompting of His Spirit, and do what He says to do in His power.

And whether that happens in a church of seventy-five or seventy-five hundred, it's still the only calling we have as Christian ministers. Ours is not an issue of size but of surrender. And that's all it ever will be.

I recently returned from South Africa, where I traveled as part of a team from the International Mission Board of my denomination. Servants of God were there from Botswana, Angola, Mozambique, Madagascar, the islands of the Indian Ocean, all over the place. Some of the precious pastors whose smiles lit up those meetings with the refreshing grace of God served churches of ten, twenty, maybe forty people who attended on a normal Sunday.

I guarantee you, these men are not concerned about multimedia classrooms and computer mice. Their hearts are for the people God has given them in some of the most remote areas of the world. All they need they already have in Christ.

And so do we. God never calls us or directs us but that He doesn't provide for us all that is necessary to follow Him.

So when you get discouraged because you're not seeing the results you want to see—but you know you're doing all God has led you to do, and you know you're walking with Him in an open, honest relationship—then let your ministry be what He wants it to be. Who's to say it's not enough? Who's to say you're coming up short or dreaming too small?

Whose opinion matters but the One who holds both you and your church squarely in His hand?

Pastors Are People Too

I'm going out on a limb here, but I'll bet some of you that have read this far aren't pastors at all.

Good. I'm glad you're still with me. Because you need to hear this too.

Ready?

Give your pastor a break. Allow him to be who God wants him to be.

I got a letter from a church once that wanted me to recommend a pastor to them. The packet came with two pages, front and back, full of suggestions that the congregation had been asked to brainstorm and write down. The letter listed everything they wanted to see in a new minister, from the most significant matters to the most incidental. It was really something!

I wrote back to tell them that I would for sure be praying for them, trusting God to send them the right man. I did tack on one little stinger to my response, though. "For the time being, however," I said, "I don't see how Jesus Himself could meet your criteria."

I'm not saying for one minute that pastors shouldn't be held to high standards. We certainly should! But the highest standard we should be held to is this: Are we being who God created us to be?

What I mean is, grace should go both ways. Thinking back to what we were just talking about in terms of church size and ministry scope, pastors simply must allow their congregations to be what God has called them to be. Not every church is supposed to be a carbon copy of all the others, and not every program that's successful in one place is ordained of God for *every* place. We should actively extend grace to our church and its people, letting God do the work of changing hearts and growing lives.

But at the same time, dear church member—dear brother or sister in Christ—please let your pastor be who God has called him to be. Extend the same kind of grace to him that you expect in return.

I know personally of a congregation who literally loved their pastor right into this message. They saw the frustration he was feeling, the mistakes he was making, the difficulties he was having. They knew he was trying to be all things to all people. But instead of railing at him and talking about him behind his back, instead of stirring up discord and silently trying to force him out, they prayed for him. They loved him. They opened their hearts to let Christ minister to him through them.

You talk about watching God heal a church and take hold of its people and its leaders! The Lord led them through their hard times, establishing His character in them, and no one within range of that church's influence could deny that Christ had done something special there . . . and is still doing it!

That's because they gave His grace room to work. They put the responsibility for change on Christ's shoulders. And in return they experienced a new bond and unity they could never have achieved on their own.

So I'm telling you, don't be shocked that your pastor has weak spots . . . just like you do. But love him in the midst of his failures. And let the grace of Christ do its job in His own redemptive way.

My own son, who now serves with me on our church staff, once said to me, "Dad, I met [a well-known Christian speaker] the other day. He said he knows you. But he wouldn't give me the time of day. Tell me, how can God use a man like that?"

"Steven," I said, "that's not the question. The *real* question is: How can God use *any* of us?"

But He does.

That's because He knows who we are. And He knows who we're not. He takes us, frail and fragile and much too fleshly, and He chisels away at all those things that interrupt the pure flow of His righteousness in our lives. The reason He goes to all this trouble is because of His earnest desire to be seen through our lives. That's why He keeps after us. That's why He keeps working on us. That's why He doesn't let up until He's transformed us.

And there's simply no other explanation for it but the loving grace of God.

I've been told—sometimes in no uncertain terms!—that there are many more things in the Bible besides this message of *Living Grace*. And I totally agree. But I firmly believe that the well from which everything in Scripture flows is the active, pursuing, life-changing reality of God's grace. If we get out of balance there—either by not giving it or not receiving it—the disharmony this causes can ripple over into all the other areas of our lives.

So let's all realize that we're nothing without the presence of God's grace in our hearts—pastors or not. And let's submit everything we are into His plan and purpose for us, so that God gets all the glory . . . and we get to live in the glow.

That really ought to be more than enough for us, don't you think?